108TH CONGRESS
1st Session

H. DOC.
108–94

OUR AMERICAN GOVERNMENT

2003 Edition

Printed by authority of H. Con. Res. 139, 108th Congress

U.S. GOVERNMENT PRINTING OFFICE

87–102 WASHINGTON : 2003

For sale by the Superintendent of Documents, U.S. Government Printing Office
Internet: bookstore.gpo.gov Phone: toll free (866) 512–1800; DC area (202) 512–1800
Fax: (202) 512–2250 Mail: Stop SSOP, Washington, DC 20402–0001

H. Con. Res. 139 Agreed to June 20, 2003

One Hundred Eighth Congress
of the
United States of America

AT THE FIRST SESSION

Begun and held at the City of Washington on Tuesday, the seventh day of January, two thousand and three

Concurrent Resolution

Resolved by the House of Representatives (the Senate concurring),

SEC. 2. OUR AMERICAN GOVERNMENT.

(a) IN GENERAL.—The 2003 revised edition of the brochure entitled "Our American Government" shall be printed as a House document under the direction of the Joint Committee on Printing.

(b) ADDITIONAL COPIES.—In addition to the usual number, there shall be printed the lesser of—

(1) 550,000 copies of the document, of which 440,000 copies shall be for the use of the House of Representatives, 100,000 copies shall be for the use of the Senate, and 10,000 copies shall be for the use of the Joint Committee on Printing; or

(2) such number of copies of the document as does not exceed a total production and printing cost of $454,160, with distribution to be allocated in the same proportion as described in paragraph (1), except that in no case shall the number of copies be less than 1 per Member of Congress.

Attest:

JEFF TRANDAHL,
Clerk of the House of Representatives.

Attest:

EMILY J. REYNOLDS,
Secretary of the Senate.

CONTENTS

FOREWORD

The Committee on House Administration is pleased to present this revised book on our United States Government.

This publication continues to be a popular introductory guide for American citizens and those of other countries who seek a greater understanding of our heritage of democracy. The question-and-answer format covers a broad range of topics dealing with the legislative, executive, and judicial branches of our Government as well as the electoral process and the role of political parties.

ROBERT W. NEY,
Chairman.

SAXBY CHAMBLISS,
Vice Chairman.

OUR AMERICAN GOVERNMENT

DEMOCRACY AND ITS AMERICAN INTERPRETATION

1. What is the purpose of the U.S. Government?

The purpose is expressed in the preamble to the Constitution: "We the People of the United States, in Order to form a more perfect Union, establish Justice, insure domestic Tranquility, provide for the common defense, promote the general Welfare, and secure the Blessings of Liberty to ourselves and our Posterity, do ordain and establish this Constitution for the United States of America."

2. What form of government do we have in the United States?

The United States, under its Constitution, is a federal, representative, democratic republic, an indivisible union of 50 sovereign States. With the exception of town meetings, a form of pure democracy, we have at the local, state, and national levels a government which is: "federal" because power is shared among these three levels; "democratic" because the people govern themselves and have the means to control the government; and "republic" because the people choose elected delegates by free and secret ballot.

3. What is the role of the citizen in our Government?

The United States today is even more of a participatory democracy than was envisioned by the Founders when they established a government "of the people, by the people, and for the people," as President Abraham Lincoln later described it. Along with the constitutional responsibilities which accompany citizenship, such as obeying laws and paying taxes, the citizen is afforded a wide range of rights and opportunities to influence the making of public policy by the Government.

At the most basic level, the right to vote gives the citizen a chance to help select those who will ultimately be responsible for determining public policy. Beyond casting the ballot, a citizen may actively assist in nominating and electing preferred public officials through volunteer activities and campaign donations. The participation of citizens in the electoral process contributes greatly to the sense of legitimacy of the Government.

Citizen involvement in the Government need not be manifested only during election campaigns. Legislators are accustomed to hearing from constituents expressing opinions about issues of the day, and procedures exist that mandate that executive agencies allow time for public comment before proposed regulations become final. Individuals may also join with others who hold similar views to make the most of their influence with Government on particular issues; this is how interest groups or political action committees are established and the lobbying process begins.

4. What contributions has our country made to the institution of government?

Some of the U.S. contributions to the institution of government are as follows: a written constitution, an independent judiciary to interpret the Constitution, and a division of powers between the Federal and State Governments.

THE CONSTITUTION

5. What is the Constitution?

The Constitution is the basic and supreme law of the United States. It prescribes the structure of the U.S. Government, provides the legal foundation on which all its actions must rest, and enumerates and guarantees the rights due all its citizens.

The Constitution is a document prepared by a convention of delegates from 12 of the 13 States that met at Philadelphia in 1787. The original charter, which replaced the Articles of Confederation and which became operative in 1789, established the United States as a federal union of States, a representative democracy within a republic. The framers provided a Government of three independent branches. The first is the legislature, which comprises a two-house or bicameral Congress consisting of a Senate, whose Members are apportioned equally among the States, and a House of Representatives, whose Members are apportioned among the States according to population. The second, the executive branch, includes the President and Vice President and all subordinate officials of the executive departments and executive agencies. The third branch, the judiciary, consists of the Supreme Court and various subordinate Federal courts created by public law.

The 27 amendments approved since 1791 are also an integral part of the Constitution. These include amendments 1 through 10, known collectively as the Bill of Rights, and amendments 11 through 27, which address a wide range of subjects. At the present time, four amendments without ratification deadlines are pending before the States. These deal with congressional apportionment, child labor, titles of nobility from foreign powers, and certain States rights (in a pre-Civil War proposal). In addition, the ratification deadlines expired on two proposed amendments, which had been approved by Congress in the 1970s: *i.e.*, equal rights for women and men and voting representation for the District of Columbia in the Senate and House.

6. What were the basic principles on which the Constitution was framed?

The framers of the Constitution debated and agreed to the following six basic principles:

1. That all States would be equal. The National Government cannot give special privileges to one State.

2. That there should be three branches of Government—one to make the laws, another to execute them, and a third to interpret them.

3. That the Government is a government of laws, not of men. No one is above the law. No officer of the Government can use authority unless and except as the Constitution or public law permits.

4. That all men are equal before the law and that anyone, rich or poor, can demand the protection of the law.

5. That the people can change the authority of the Government by changing (amending) the Constitution. (One such change provided for the election of Senators by direct popular vote instead of by State legislatures).

6. That the Constitution, and the laws of the United States and treaties made pursuant to it, are "the supreme Law of the Land."

7. What is the Bill of Rights?

The Bill of Rights is a series of constitutionally protected rights of citizens. The first 10 amendments to the Constitution, ratified by the required number of States on December 15, 1791, are commonly referred to as the Bill of Rights. The first eight amendments set out or enumerate the substantive and procedural individual rights associated with that description. The 9th and 10th amendments are general rules of interpretation of the relationships among the people, the State governments, and the Federal Government. The ninth amendment provides that the "enumeration in the Constitution, of certain rights, shall not be construed to deny or disparage others retained by the people." The 10th amendment reads: "The powers not delegated to the United States by the Constitution, nor prohibited by it to the States, are reserved to the States respectively, or to the people."

8. What are the rights enumerated in the Bill of Rights?

Right to freedom of religion, speech, and press (Amendment I);

Right to assemble peaceably, and to petition the Government for a redress of grievances (Amendment I);

Right to keep and bear arms in common defense (Amendment II);

Right not to have soldiers quartered in one's home in peacetime without the consent of the owner, nor in time of war except as prescribed by law (Amendment III);

Right to be secure against "unreasonable searches and seizures" (Amendment IV);

Right in general not to be held to answer criminal charges except upon indictment by a grand jury (Amendment V);

Right not to be put twice in jeopardy for the same offense (Amendment V);

Right not to be compelled to be a witness against oneself in a criminal case (Amendment V);

Right not to be deprived of life, liberty, or property without due process of law (Amendment V);

Right to just compensation for private property taken for public use (Amendment V);

Right in criminal prosecution to a speedy and public trial by an impartial jury, to be informed of the charges, to be confronted with witnesses, to have a compulsory process for calling witnesses in defense of the accused, and to have legal counsel (Amendment VI);

Right to a jury trial in suits at common law involving over $20 (Amendment VII);

Right not to have excessive bail required, nor excessive fines imposed, nor cruel and unusual punishments inflicted (Amendment VIII).

9. How may the Constitution be amended?

Amending the Constitution involves two separate processes.

First, amendments may be proposed on the initiative of Congress (by two-thirds affirmative vote in each House) or by convention (on application of two-thirds of the State legislatures). So far, a convention has never been called.

The second step is ratification of a proposed amendment. At the discretion of Congress, Congress may designate ratification either by the State legislatures or by conventions. Ratification requires approval by three-fourths of the States. Out of the 27 amendments, only one (the 21st, ending Prohibition) has been ratified by State conventions.

The first 10 amendments (ratified in 1791) were practically a part of the original instrument. The 11th amendment was ratified in 1795, and the 12th amendment in 1804. Thereafter, no amendment was made to the Constitution for 60 years. Shortly after the Civil War, three amendments were ratified (1865–70), followed by another long interval before the 16th amendment became effective in 1913. The most recent amendment, the 27th, was ratified on May 7, 1992. At the present time, there are four amendments pending before the States that were proposed without ratification deadlines.

10. How long may a proposed amendment to the Constitution remain outstanding and open to ratification?

The Supreme Court has stated that ratification must be within "some reasonable time after the proposal." Beginning with the 18th amendment, it has been customary for Congress to set a definite period for ratification. In the case of the 18th, 20th, 21st, and 22nd amendments, the period set was 7 years, but there has been no determination as to just how long a "reasonable time" might extend.

In the case of the proposed equal rights amendment, the Congress extended the ratification period from 7 to approximately 10 years; but the proposed Amendment was never ratified.

The "reasonable time" doctrine recently arose, as well, in connection with an amendment pertaining to congressional pay, proposed in 1789 without a ratification deadline. The 38th State, Michigan, ratified this amendment on May 7, 1992–203 years after its proposal. The amendment was certified by the Archivist of the United States, since it did not carry a term limitation, as the 27th Amendment to the Constitution.

11. What is the "lame duck" amendment?

The "lame duck" amendment is the popular name for the 20th amendment to the Constitution, ratified on February 6, 1933. It is designed to limit the time that elected officials can serve after the general election in November. This amendment provides, among other things, that the terms of the President and Vice President end at noon on January 20, the terms of Senators and Representatives end at noon on January 3, and the terms of their successors then begin.

Prior to this amendment, the annual session of Congress began on the first Monday in December (Article 1, Section 4). Since the terms of new Members formerly did not begin until March 4, Members who had been defeated or did not stand for reelection in November continued to serve during the lame duck session from December until March 4. Adoption of the 20th amendment has reduced but not eliminated legislation by a Congress that does not represent the latest choice of the people. For instance, 11 of the 33 Congresses from 1933 to 1999 (73rd through the 105th Congress) continued to meet after the November general elections.

12. Have any amendments to the Constitution been repealed?

Only one, the 18th amendment (Prohibition), ratified in early 1919, was repealed by the 21st amendment in late 1933.

13. What is meant by the "separation of powers" and "checks and balances" in the Federal Government?

The separation of powers and checks and balances are two fundamental principles underlying the Constitution. They work together to prevent a tyrannous concentration of power in any one branch, to check and restrain Government, and, ultimately, to protect the rights and liberties of citizens.

The Constitution contains provisions in separate articles for the three branches of Government—legislative, executive, and judicial. There is a significant difference in the grants of authority to these branches, each of which is also given an independent base of political power. The First Article, dealing with legislative power, vests in Congress "All legislative Powers herein granted"; the Second Article vests "The executive Power" in the President; and the Third Article states that "The judicial Power of the United States shall be vested in one Supreme Court, and in such inferior Courts as the Congress may from time to time ordain and establish." In addition to this separation and independence among the three branches, the Constitution sets up "auxiliary precautions," as James Madison called them in the Federalist Papers, that allow each branch to check and balance the others. For instance, the President can veto bills approved by Congress and nominates individuals to the Federal judiciary; the Supreme Court can declare a law enacted by Congress or an action by the President unconstitutional; and Congress can impeach and remove the President and Federal court justices and judges.

THE LEGISLATIVE BRANCH

THE CONGRESS

14. What is Congress?

The Congress of the United States is the legislative (lawmaking) and oversight (Government policy review) body of our National Government, and consists of two Houses—the Senate and the House of Representatives.

MEMBERS, OFFICES, AND STAFF

15. What qualifications are prescribed for a Member of Congress?

The Constitution (Article 1, Section 2 for the House and Section 3 for the Senate) prescribes qualifications for Members of Congress.

A Member of the House of Representatives must be at least 25 years of age when entering office, must have been a U.S. citizen for at least seven years, and must be a resident of the State in which the election occurred.

A Member of the U.S. Senate must be at least 30 years of age to enter office, must have been a U.S. citizen for nine years, and must be a resident of the State in which the election occurred.

16. What is the term of a Congress and how often must it meet?

A Congress begins at noon, January 3 of each odd-numbered year following a general election, unless by law a different day is designated. A Congress lasts for two years, with each year normally constituting a separate session.

The Legislative Reorganization Act of 1970 requires Congress to adjourn sine die not later than July 31 of each year unless there is a declared war, or unless Congress otherwise provides. In odd-numbered years, Congress must take an August recess if it fails to adjourn by July 31.

Neither the House nor the Senate may adjourn for more than three days (excluding Saturdays, Sundays, and holidays) without the concurrence of the other Chamber. It has also become a common practice for Congress to adjourn after making provision for the House and Senate leaders to summon Congress back into session in emergency circumstances. Similarly, the Constitution grants the President the authority to summon the Congress for a special session if circumstances require.

17. How many Members does each State have in the Senate and House of Representatives?

Each State, under the Constitution, is entitled to two Senators, each serving a six-year term, and at least one Representative, serving a two-year term. Additional House seats are apportioned on the basis of State population. (See State Population and House Apportionment table in Appendix.)

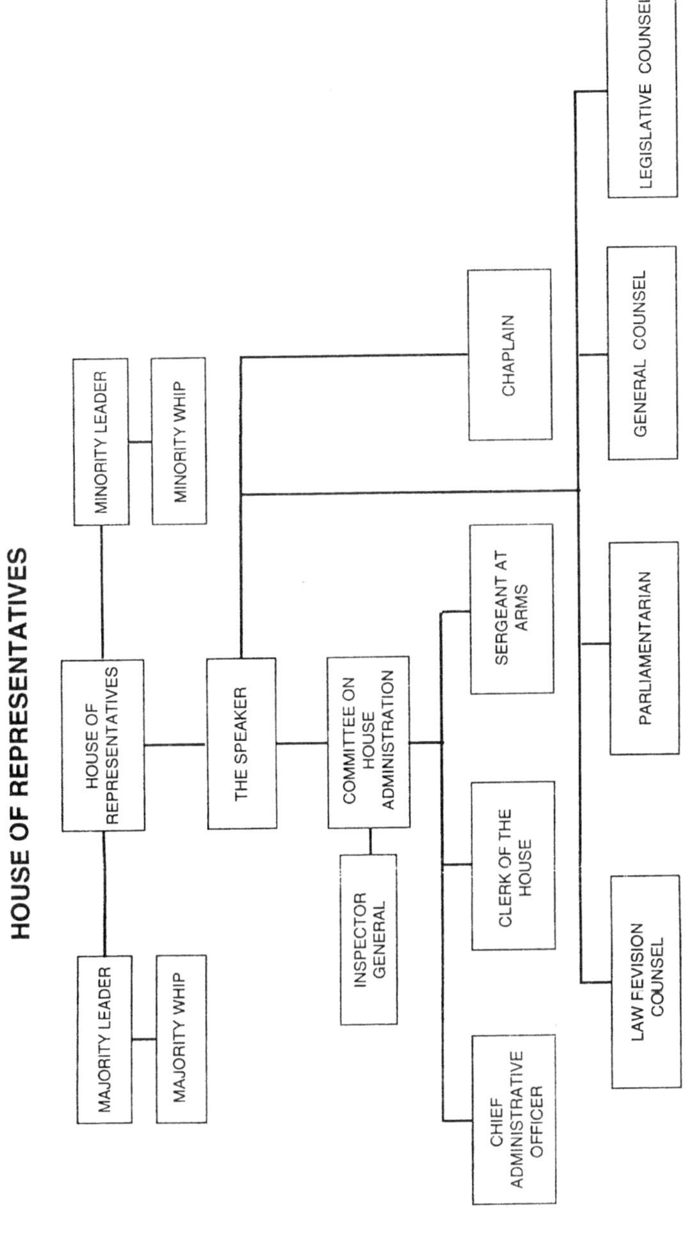
HOUSE OF REPRESENTATIVES
MAJORITY LEADER
MAJORITY WHIP
HOUSE OF REPRESENTATIVES
MINORITY LEADER
MINORITY WHIP
THE SPEAKER
COMMITTEE ON HOUSE ADMINISTRATION
INSPECTOR GENERAL
CHAPLAIN
CHIEF ADMINISTRATIVE OFFICER
CLERK OF THE HOUSE
SERGEANT AT ARMS
LAW FEVISION COUNSEL
PARLIAMENTARIAN
GENERAL COUNSEL
LEGISLATIVE COUNSEL

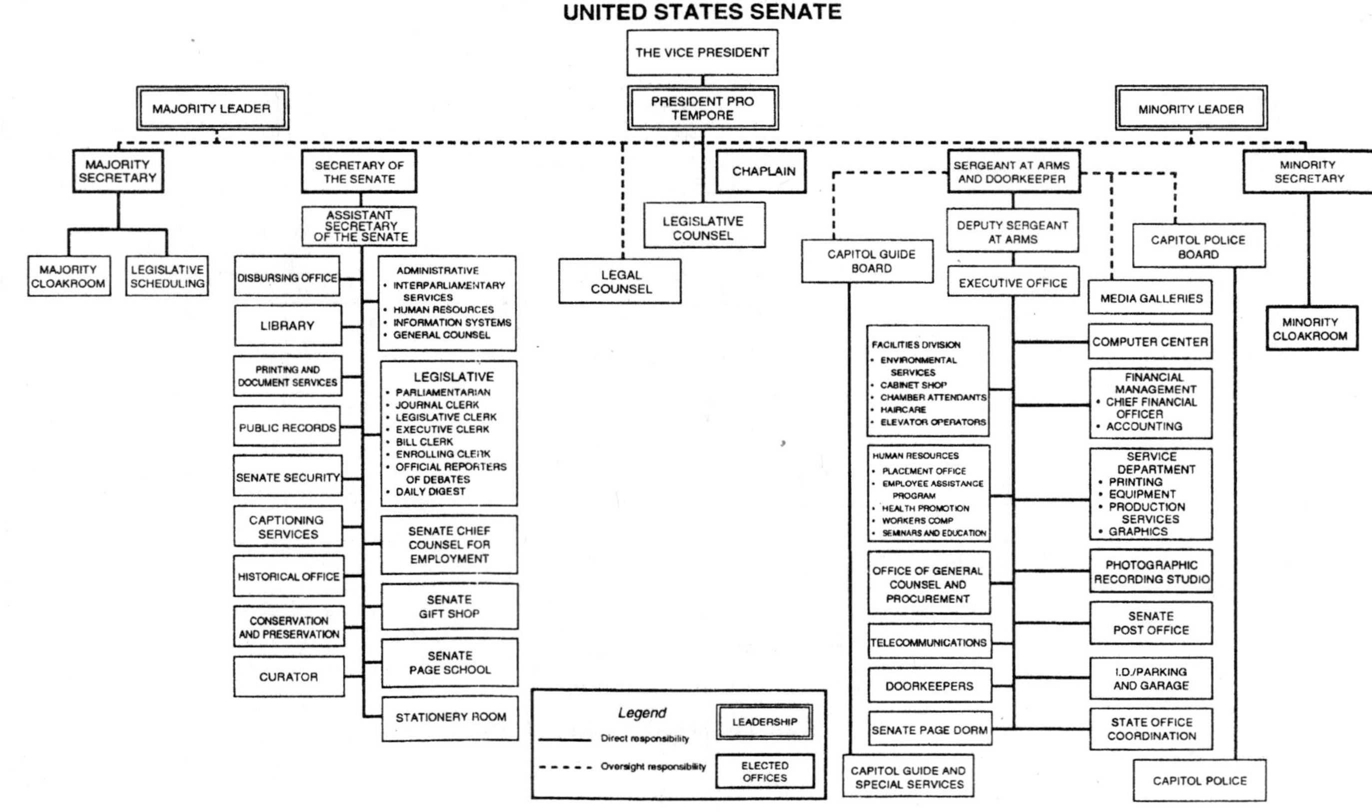
UNITED STATES SENATE
THE VICE PRESIDENT
PRESIDENT PRO TEMPORE
MAJORITY LEADER
MINORITY LEADER
MAJORITY SECRETARY
MAJORITY CLOAKROOM
LEGISLATIVE SCHEDULING
SECRETARY OF THE SENATE
ASSISTANT SECRETARY OF THE SENATE
DISBURSING OFFICE
LIBRARY
PRINTING AND DOCUMENT SERVICES
PUBLIC RECORDS
SENATE SECURITY
CAPTIONING SERVICES
HISTORICAL OFFICE
CONSERVATION AND PRESERVATION
CURATOR
ADMINISTRATIVE
• INTERPARLIAMENTARY SERVICES
• HUMAN RESOURCES
• INFORMATION SYSTEMS
• GENERAL COUNSEL
LEGISLATIVE
• PARLIAMENTARIAN
• JOURNAL CLERK
• LEGISLATIVE CLERK
• EXECUTIVE CLERK
• BILL CLERK
• ENROLLING CLERK
• OFFICIAL REPORTERS OF DEBATES
• DAILY DIGEST
SENATE CHIEF COUNSEL FOR EMPLOYMENT
SENATE GIFT SHOP
SENATE PAGE SCHOOL
STATIONERY ROOM
LEGAL COUNSEL
LEGISLATIVE COUNSEL
CHAPLAIN
SERGEANT AT ARMS AND DOORKEEPER
DEPUTY SERGEANT AT ARMS
EXECUTIVE OFFICE
CAPITOL GUIDE BOARD
CAPITOL POLICE BOARD
FACILITIES DIVISION
• ENVIRONMENTAL SERVICES
• CABINET SHOP
• CHAMBER ATTENDANTS
• HAIRCARE
• ELEVATOR OPERATORS
HUMAN RESOURCES
• PLACEMENT OFFICE
• EMPLOYEE ASSISTANCE PROGRAM
• HEALTH PROMOTION
• WORKERS COMP
• SEMINARS AND EDUCATION
OFFICE OF GENERAL COUNSEL AND PROCUREMENT
TELECOMMUNICATIONS
DOORKEEPERS
SENATE PAGE DORM
CAPITOL GUIDE AND SPECIAL SERVICES
MEDIA GALLERIES
COMPUTER CENTER
FINANCIAL MANAGEMENT
• CHIEF FINANCIAL OFFICER
• ACCOUNTING
SERVICE DEPARTMENT
• PRINTING
• EQUIPMENT
• PRODUCTION SERVICES
• GRAPHICS
PHOTOGRAPHIC RECORDING STUDIO
SENATE POST OFFICE
I.D./PARKING AND GARAGE
STATE OFFICE COORDINATION
CAPITOL POLICE
MINORITY SECRETARY
MINORITY CLOAKROOM
Legend
Direct responsibility
Oversight responsibility
LEADERSHIP
ELECTED OFFICES

18. What is the size of the House of Representatives and how is it determined?

The membership of the House of Representatives is fixed in law at 435 Members representing the 50 States. In addition to the 435 Representatives, there is one Delegate for each of the following: the District of Columbia, the Virgin Islands, Guam, and American Samoa (each elected for a two-year term); as well as a Resident Commissioner from Puerto Rico (elected for a four-year term). The Delegates and the Resident Commissioner can sponsor legislation and vote in committees, but not in the House Chamber.

The Constitution entitles each State to at least one Representative. Beyond this minimum, Representatives are apportioned among the States according to population. Population figures used for apportionment are determined on the basis of each 10-year census. (Following the 1990 census, the average district size was about 570,000 people). Since 1941, Congress has used the method of "equal proportions" to calculate actual apportionment, in order to minimize the differences in district populations among the States.

19. Who defines the congressional districts—the Federal Government or the States?

Congress fixes the size of the House of Representatives, and the procedure for apportioning the number of Representatives among the States, and the States themselves proceed from there. State legislatures pass laws defining the physical boundaries of congressional districts, within certain constraints established by Congress and the Supreme Court (through its reapportionment and redistricting rulings). Each State is apportioned its number of Representatives by means of the Department of Commerce's decennial census.

In the very early years of the Republic, most States elected their Representatives at large. The practice of dividing a State into districts, however, was soon instituted. Congress later required that Representatives be elected from "districts composed of a contiguous and compact territory," but this requirement is no longer in Federal law.

The redistricting process has always been provided for by State law, but Congress can choose to exercise greater authority over redistricting. In 1967, for example, Congress by law prohibited at-large elections of Representatives in all States entitled to more than one Representative. Today, all States with more than one Representative must elect their Representatives from single-Member districts.

20. What is a Member of Congress?

A Member of Congress is a person serving in the Senate or the House of Representatives. A Member of the Senate is referred to as Senator, and a Member of the House of Representatives, as Representative or Congressman or Congresswoman.

21. What is a Delegate or Resident Commissioner, as distinguished from a Representative?

The office of Delegate was established by ordinance from the Continental Congress (1774–89) and confirmed by a law of Congress. From the beginning of the Republic, accordingly, the House of Representatives has admitted Delegates from Territories or districts organized by law. Delegates and Resident Commissioners may participate in House debate but they are not permitted to vote on the floor. All serve on committees of the House and possess powers and privileges equal to other Members in committee, including the right to vote in committee. Currently, there are four Delegates in the House and one Resident Commissioner.

22. What oath of office is required for Members of Congress, and when is it administered?

Article VI of the U.S. Constitution requires that Members of Congress, and all executive and judicial officers, shall be bound by oath or affirmation to support the Constitution. The oath of office is as follows: *"I, AB, solemnly swear (or affirm) that I will support and defend the Constitution of the United States against all enemies, foreign or domestic; that I will bear true faith and allegiance to the same; that I take this obligation freely, without any mental reservation or purpose of evasion; and that I will well and faithfully discharge the duties of the office on which I am about to enter. So help me God."*

Representatives take the oath of office on the first day of the new Congress, immediately after the House has elected and sworn in its Speaker. Those Senators elected or reelected the previous November take the oath of office as the first item of business when the Senate convenes the following January. Representatives elected in special elections during the course of a Congress, and Senators appointed or elected to fill a vacancy in the Senate, generally take the oath of office on the floor of their respective Chamber when the Clerk of the House or the Secretary of the Senate has received formal notice of the new Member's election or appointment from State government authorities. On rare occasions, because of illness or other circumstances, a Member-elect has been authorized to take the oath of office at a place other than the House or Senate Chamber. In those circumstances, the Clerk of the House or Secretary of the Senate sees to the proper administration of the oath.

23. In the event of the death, resignation, or declination (refusal to serve) of a Member of Congress, how is the vacancy filled?

The Constitution (Article II, Section 2, Clause 4) requires that all vacancies in the House of Representatives be filled by election. All States require special elections to fill any House seat that becomes vacant during the First Session of a Congress. Procedures governing vacancies occurring during the Second Session of a Congress differ from State to State, and are largely dependent on the amount of time intervening between the vacancy and the next general election.

In the Senate, when a vacancy occurs for any reason, the 17th Amendment directs the Governor of the State to call an election to fill such vacancy, and authorizes the legislature to make provision for an immediate appointment pending such election. Among the States, only Arizona and Wisconsin do not allow the Governor to make interim appointments, requiring, instead, a special election to fill any Senate vacancy. Prevailing practice in the States is that a special election to fill the vacancy is scheduled to be held at the time of the next statewide general election.

24. How can Members of Congress be removed from office or punished for misconduct?

It is generally understood in Congress that the impeachment process stipulated in the Constitution, which involves both House and Senate actions, applies only to the removal of the President, Vice President, Supreme Court Justices, and Federal judges, and civil officers of the U.S. Government, and not to the removal of Members of Congress from office. The Constitution states that "Each House shall be the Judge of the . . . Qualifications of its own Members . . . [and may] punish its Members for disorderly Behaviour, and with the Concurrence of two thirds, expel a Member." Thus, disciplinary actions taken against a Member are a matter of concern for that House acting alone.

Each Chamber has established a committee charged with reviewing allegations of misconduct against its Members: the House Committee on Standards of Official Conduct and the Senate Ethics Committee. The Rules of the House and Senate also contain a Code of Official Conduct. The ethics committees review charges against a Member filed by another Member or by a private citizen.

The most severe punishment that can be imposed by either the House or Senate is the expulsion of the offending Member. This action requires, constitutionally, an affirmative vote of two-thirds of the Members of the Chamber voting, a quorum being present. Alternatively, the House may vote to "censure" a Member for misconduct. This requires only a majority vote, and, under party rules in the House, a censured Member automatically loses any committee or party leadership positions held during that Congress. In the Senate, the terms "censure" and "denunciation" are used almost interchangeably for violations of this magnitude.

A less severe form of disciplinary action in both the House and Senate is a "reprimand," again imposed by a Chamber by a simple majority vote. Typically, reprimands are reserved for ethical violations that are minor, or appear to be inadvertent or unintentional on the part of the Member.

Additionally, Members of Congress are subject to prosecution for treason, felony, or breach of the peace. Generally, when a Member has been indicted for a felony, a "leave of absence" from any party or committee leadership position must be taken so long as the charges are pending. Usually, the House or Senate will not initiate internal disciplinary action until the criminal proceedings against the Member have been completed.

25. Are Members of Congress, to some extent, privileged from arrest?

Article 1, Section 6 of the Constitution states that Senators and Representatives "shall in all Cases, except Treason, Felony, and Breach of the Peace, be privileged from Arrest during their Attendance at the Session of their respective Houses, and in going to and returning from the same." The phrase "Treason, Felony, and Breach of the Peace" has been construed to mean all indictable crimes, and the Supreme Court has held that the privilege against arrest does not apply in any criminal cases.

26. Who are the officers of the House and how are they chosen?

Elected officers include the Speaker, Clerk, Sergeant at Arms, Chief Administrative Officer (CAO), and Chaplain. Another officer, the Inspector General, is appointed jointly by the Speaker, Majority Leader, and Minority Leader. Each of these officers appoints the employees provided by law for his or her department. (For an overview of the House's leadership and administrative structure, see the accompanying graphic, House of Representatives.)

The Constitution (Article 1, Section 2) says that the House "shall chuse [sic] their Speaker and other officers"; i.e., the Members vote as they do on any other question, except that in most cases it is strictly a party vote. Republicans and Democrats both meet before the House organizes for a new Congress, and choose a slate of officers. These two slates are presented at the first session of the House, and the majority-party slate can be expected to be selected. Traditionally, the majority party's nominee for Chaplain is not contested. The nominees for Clerk, Sergeant at Arms, CAO, and Chaplain are elected by a tally recorded by the House's electronic voting machine. For election of the Speaker, Members' names are called alphabetically, and they respond by orally stating the name of the candidate they prefer.

27. What are the duties of the officers and senior officials of the House?

The officers and officials of the House are, except where noted, elected by the House at the beginning of each Congress. They are the principal managers for the House of essential legislative, financial, administrative, and security functions. Their duties are prescribed in House Rule II and in statutes.

The Clerk of the House.—The Clerk is the chief legislative officer of the House. After each election, the Clerk receives the credentials of newly elected Members and presides at the opening of each new Congress pending the election of a Speaker. The Clerk keeps the official Journal of House proceedings, certifies all votes, and signs all bills and resolutions that have passed the House. The Clerk's office supervises the enrollment of legislation which originated in the House, and its presentment to the President. The Clerk's office also supervises legislative information resources in the House, the page program, and units providing public documents to the press and public.

The Sergeant at Arms.—The Sergeant at Arms is responsible for maintaining order on the floor and in the galleries when the House is in session. The office also maintains security in the House side of the Capitol and in House office buildings and facilities. As part of this responsibility, the House Sergeant at Arms, along with his or her Senate counterpart and the Architect of the Capitol, comprise the Capitol Police Board and the Capitol Guide Board. In addition, the Sergeant at Arms is charged with carrying out Section 5 of Article I of the Constitution, which authorizes the House (and Senate) "to compel the Attendance of absent Members."

The Chaplain.—The House Chaplain opens each daily House session with a prayer and provides pastoral services to House Members, their families, and staff. He also arranges for visits by guest chaplains. Traditionally, the Chaplain retains his post when party control of the House changes.

The Chief Administrative Officer (CAO).—The CAO is the principal House officer responsible for the financial management of House of Representatives accounts. Quarterly, his office issues a public document identifying all expenditures made by House Members, committees, and officers from appropriated funds at their disposal. The CAO's office, in addition to its financial management responsibilities, provides a range of services to Member and committee offices, including telecommunications, postal, and computer services, office supply and maintenance services, payroll and accounting services, employee counseling and assistance programs, and supervises private vendors and contractors providing services to the House.

The Inspector General (IG).—The Inspector General is the chief investigative officer of the House. His office (either through its own staff or through consultants) conducts periodic audits of House financial and administrative offices and operations. The IG's findings and recommendations are submitted to the appropriate House offices, to the congressional leadership, and to the House Administration Committee. The IG serves a two-year term and is jointly appointed by the Speaker, the Majority Leader, and the Minority Leader.

The General Counsel.—The General Counsel is the chief legal advisor to the House, its leaders and officers, and to its Members. The office represents the House, its Members, or employees in litigation resulting from the performance of official duties. The General Counsel is appointed by the Speaker in consultation with a bipartisan legal advisory group, which includes the Majority and Minority leaders.

The Historian.—By statute, the Office of the Historian acts to preserve the historical records of the House and its Members, to encourage historical research on the House, and to undertake original research and writing on the history of the House. The Historian is appointed by the Speaker. When the post is vacant, other legislative branch organizations and offices may perform some of these services and functions.

28. What are the duties of the Speaker?

The Speaker presides over the House, appoints chairmen to preside over the Committee of the Whole, appoints all special or select committees, appoints conference committees, has the power of recognition of Members to speak, and makes many important rulings and decisions in the House. The Speaker may vote, but usually does not, except in case of a tie. The Speaker and the Majority Leader determine the legislative agenda for the House and often confer with the President and with the Senate leadership.

29. Could a person other than an elected Representative in Congress serve as Speaker of the House?

Technically, yes. There is no constitutional impediment to such a selection. The House is empowered to choose its Speaker and other officers without restriction. But this possibility is unlikely, and indeed, the Speaker has always been a Member of the House.

30. Who was the Speaker of the House of Representatives for the longest period of time?

Sam Rayburn, of Texas, who was a Member of the House for 48 years and 8 months, served as Speaker for 17 years and 2 months. However, the record for longest continuous service as Speaker is held by Thomas P. "Tip" O'Neill, of Massachusetts, who served consecutively for 10 years, thus surpassing John McCormack (8 years, 11 months, and 23 days); Champ Clark (7 years, 10 months, and 29 days); and Joseph G. Cannon (7 years, 3 months, and 24 days).

31. Who presides over the Senate?

The Constitution provides that "the Vice President of the United States shall be the President of the Senate" (Article 1, section 3). As President of the Senate, the Vice President presides over the Senate, makes parliamentary rulings (which may be overturned by a majority vote of the Senate or by supermajority, 60 votes, in certain instances), and may cast tie-breaking votes. At first, Vice Presidents presided on a regular basis, but in recent years they are present in the chair only when a close vote is anticipated, during major debates, or on important ceremonial occasions (such as the swearing in of newly elected Senators, or during joint sessions). In the absence of the Vice President, the Senate elects a President pro tempore (president "for the time being") to preside. In recent decades it has become traditional for this post to go to the senior Senator from the majority party. The President pro tempore assigns other Members of the majority party to preside by rotation during each day's proceedings. These Senators and the President pro tempore retain their rights to vote on all issues before the body and to debate when they are not presiding.

32. Who are the officers of the Senate, how are they chosen, and what are their duties?

By resolution, the Senate elects five officers: the Secretary, Sergeant at Arms, Chaplain, Secretary for the Majority, and Secretary for the Minority. (For an overview of the Senate's leadership and administrative structure, see the accompanying graphic, United States Senate.)

Secretary of the Senate.—As the Senate's chief administrative officer, the Secretary supervises offices and services supporting the Senate's day-to-day operations, including those of the Parliamentarian and the legislative and executive business clerks responsible for processing legislative documentation. Among the other offices supervised by the Secretary are the Senate Library, the Senate Historical Office, curatorial and conservation offices, and the offices of the reporters of debates and of the Daily Digest. The Secretary officially certifies the bills and resolutions passed by the Senate, records Senator's oaths of office, records the registration of lobbyists, and administers the Federal election records required to be filed by senatorial candidates.

Sergeant at Arms.—The Sergeant at Arms is the chief law enforcement and security officer of the Senate, charged with enforcing Senate rules and regulations in the Chamber, and in Senate office buildings. The Sergeant at Arms implements orders of the Senate, including locating absent Senators and, when so directed, making arrests. The Sergeant at Arms notified President Andrew Johnson in 1868 and President William Jefferson Clinton in 1999 of impeachment charges to be tried in the Senate. As the Senate's protocol officer, the Sergeant at Arms escorts the President and other dignitaries during official visits to the Capitol, leads formal processions during Senate ceremonies, and arranges funerals for Senators who die in office. The Sergeant at Arms supervises many Senate support services, including the Senate Computer Center; the Service Department; Senate postal and telecommunications services, gallery services including pages, media galleries and services, recording studios, doorkeepers, and Capitol tour guides, among others.

Secretary for the Majority.—Generally nominated by the Majority Leader with the approval of the majority conference (the organizational body of all majority party senators), the Secretary for the Majority oversees party activities in the Senate Chamber and the majority cloakroom. The Secretary supervises telephone pages and messengers, organizes meetings of the majority conference, briefs Senators and staff on pending measures and votes, and conducts polls of Senators when requested by party leaders to determine Senators' views on scheduling issues and pending Senate business.

Secretary for the Minority.—The Secretary for the Minority is chosen in the same manner as is the majority secretary, that is, by the minority leadership and conference. The duties of the post are essentially the same as those of the majority party secretary.

Chaplain.—Nominated in the conference of the majority-party Senators, the full Senate elects the Senate Chaplain. The Chaplain prepares and offers the convening prayer each day the Senate is in session; provides pastoral services to Senators, their families and staffs; and supervises the scheduling of appearances by guest chaplains. Traditionally, changes in party control do not interrupt the tenure of the Chaplain of the Senate.

33. What are party Leaders?

The political parties in the House and Senate elect Leaders to represent them on the floor, to advocate their policies and viewpoints, to coordinate their legislative efforts, and to help determine the schedule of legislative business. The Leaders serve as spokespersons for their parties and for the House and Senate as a whole. Since the Framers of the Constitution did not anticipate political parties, these leadership posts are not defined in the Constitution but have evolved over time. The House, with its larger membership, required Majority and Minority Leaders in the 19th century to expedite legislative business and to keep their parties united. The Senate did not formally designate party floor leaders until the 1920s, although several caucus chairmen and committee chairmen had previously performed similar duties. In both Houses, the parties also elect assistant leaders, or "Whips." The Majority Leader is elected by the majority-party conference (or caucus), the Minority Leader by the minority-party conference. Third parties have rarely had enough members to need to elect their own leadership, and independents will generally join one of the larger party organizations to receive committee assignments. Majority and Minority Leaders receive a higher salary than other Members in recognition of their additional responsibilities.

34. Are the Majority Leaders elected by their respective Houses of Congress?

No. Rather, Members of the majority party in the House, meeting in caucus or conference, select the Majority Leader. The minority-party Members, in a similar meeting, select their Minority Leader. The majority and minority parties in the Senate also hold separate meetings to elect their leaders.

35. What are the duties of the "Whips" of the Congress?

The Whips (of the majority and minority parties) keep track of all politically important legislation and endeavor to have all members of their parties present when important measures are to be voted upon. When a vote appears to be close, the Whips contact absent Members of their party, and advise them of the vote. The Whips assist the leadership in managing the party's legislative program on the floor of the Chambers and provide information to party Members about important legislative-related matters. The authority of the Whips over party Members is informal; in the U.S. Congress, a Member may vote against the position supported by a majority of the Member's party colleagues because of personal opposition or because of opposition evident within his or her constituency. In most cases, parties take no disciplinary action against colleagues who vote against the party position.

The Majority and Minority Whips in the House and Senate are elected by party Members in that Chamber. In the House, with its larger number of Members, the Majority and Minority Whips appoint deputy whips to assist them in their activities.

36. What are party caucuses or party conferences and party committees?

A party caucus or conference is the name given to a meeting, whether regular or specially called, of all party Members in the House or Senate. The term "caucus" or "conference" can also mean the organization of all party Members in the House or Senate.

House Democrats refer to their organization as a "caucus." House and Senate Republicans and Senate Democrats call their three organizations as "conferences." The caucus or conference officially elects party floor leaders, the party whips, and nominates each party's candidates for the Speakership or President pro tempore and other officers in the House or Senate. The chairs of the party conferences and other subordinate party leaders are elected by vote of the conference or caucus at the beginning of each Congress. Regular caucus or conference meetings provide a forum in which party leaders and rank-and-file party Members can discuss party policy, pending legislative issues, and other matters of mutual concern.

The party caucus or conference also traditionally establishes party committees with specialized functions. Party committees generally nominate party Members to serve on the various committees of the House or Senate, subject to approval by the caucus or conference. Policy committees generally discuss party positions on pending legislation. Steering committees generally plan the schedule of Chamber action on pending legislation. Research committees conduct studies on broad policy questions, generally before committees of the House or Senate begin action on legislation. Campaign committees provide research and strategy assistance to party candidates for election to the House or Senate. The chairs of party committees are generally elected by their respective party caucus or conference; the exception is the House Democratic Steering and Policy Committee, which is chaired by the Speaker of the House (when the Democrats are in the majority) or by the Democratic floor leader (when they are in the minority).

The caucus or conference may also decide to appoint "task forces" to perform research on a new policy proposal, or to assist the formal leadership in developing a party position on important legislation. These "task forces" are traditionally disbanded once their work has been completed.

37. What are caucuses, congressional Member organizations, and other similar groups?

Congressional Member Organizations (CMOs), commonly referred to as caucuses, are groups of Members of Congress formed to pursue common legislative objectives. CMOs are voluntary groups that have no legal or corporate identity. CMOs take a variety of forms: some are comprised only of House Members, some only of Senators, and some have a membership drawn from both chambers. Many CMOs are bipartisan, having both Republican and Democratic members. A number of CMOs have been organized around State or regional issues and around subjects concerned with fostering legislative attention to particular policy topics. CMOs do not receive separate offices or facilities; instead, they work out of individual Representatives' or Senators' offices, using the staff and facilities provided to Members of Congress who are active in a particular group.

38. Do Members of the House have individual seats on the Chamber floor?

Representatives had individual seats until the 63rd Congress (1913), but now Members may sit where they choose. Democrats occupy the east side of the Chamber, on the Speaker's right; Republicans sit across the main aisle, on the Speaker's left. Two tables each on the Democratic and Republican sides of the aisle are reserved for committee leaders during debate on a bill reported from their committee and for party leaders.

39. Do Senators have individual seats assigned them?

Yes. The individual seats in the Senate are numbered and assigned on request of Senators in order of their seniority. Democrats occupy the west side of the Chamber on the Vice President's right; Republicans sit across the main aisle to the Vice President's left. There is no set rule for seating of "Independents." By custom, the Majority and Minority Leaders occupy the front row seats on either side of the aisle, and the Majority and Minority Whips occupy the seats immediately next to their party's leader.

40. Do the terms "senior Senator" and "junior Senator" apply to age or service?

The words "senior" or "junior" as applied to the two Senators from a State refer to their length of continuous service in the Senate, and not to their ages. Thus, a senior Senator may be younger in age than the junior Senator from the same State.

41. What provisions are made for offices for Members and committees of the Congress?

The Capitol Hill office complex includes offices for House and Senate leaders and officers and for certain committees in the Capitol building itself, plus five House office buildings and three Senate office buildings, plus additional rented space in commercial office buildings near Union Station, north of the Capitol.

The three main House office buildings are located on Independence Avenue, south of the Capitol. Proceeding from east to west, the three buildings are the Cannon House Office Building, completed in 1908; the Longworth House Office Building, completed in 1933; and the Rayburn House Office Building, completed in 1965. The buildings are named for the Speakers of the House at the time the construction of the buildings was authorized. In these buildings are located the personal offices of each Member of the House, as well as the offices of House standing committees. Two additional buildings were purchased in 1957 and 1975 for use by the House for additional office space. The first building, on C Street behind the Cannon Office Building, was renamed the Thomas P. O'Neill House Office Building in 1990 and demolished in 2002. In addition to space for House committee and subcommittee staff, the building is now also the site of the House Page School Dormitory. The second building, on D Street SW, was renamed in 1990 the Gerald R. Ford House Office Building. Before becoming Vice President and President, Mr. Ford was House Republican Leader from 1965–73. He is the first person not to have been Speaker to have a House office building named after him.

The Senate office buildings are located on Constitution Avenue, northeast of the Capitol. The buildings were completed in 1909, 1958, and 1982, and are named in honor of influential 20th century

Senators: Richard B. Russell (D., GA), Everett M. Dirksen (R., IL), and Philip A. Hart (D., MI), respectively.

In addition to office space in Washington, DC, Representatives and Senators are entitled to rent office space in their districts or States.

42. What organizations are included in the legislative branch?

In addition to Congress—the House of Representatives and the Senate—the legislative branch includes the Architect of the Capitol, the Government Printing Office (GPO), the Library of Congress, and the legislative support agencies. The Architect's principal duties involve the construction, maintenance, and renovation of the Capitol Building as well as the congressional office buildings and other structures in the Capitol complex such as the Library of Congress buildings. GPO publishes the Congressional Record, congressional committee hearings and reports, and other congressional documents, as well as many executive branch publications. The Library of Congress, in addition to providing library services, research, and analysis to Congress, is also the national library. It houses premier national book, map, and manuscript collections in the United States; serves a major role assisting local libraries in book cataloging and other services; and supervises the implementation of U.S. copyright laws.

Three support agencies are also part of the legislative branch. The Congressional Budget Office, the Congressional Research Service in the Library of Congress, and the General Accounting Office directly assist Congress in the performance of its duties. On occasion, temporary advisory commissions are established and funded in the legislative branch.

43. What are the functions of the congressional support agencies that are funded in the legislative appropriations acts?

Legislative support agencies funded in the legislative appropriations act include the Congressional Budget Office (CBO), the Congressional Research Service (CRS) of the Library of Congress, and the General Accounting Office (GAO). CBO assists the House and Senate Budget Committees in evaluating the spending and revenue priorities of Congress and aids all congressional committees in estimating the cost of proposed legislation. CRS provides reference, research, and analytical assistance to committees, Members, and staff of Congress on current and anticipated policy issues. GAO primarily studies and reports to Congress on the economy and efficiency of Government programs, operations, and expenditures.

44. What services are officially available to Members and to committees to assist them in the performance of their legislative duties?

Research assistance is available both from congressional staff and from legislative branch agencies created to assist Members, committees, and their staffs.

Senators and Representatives are allocated funds to hire personal staff to assist them in performance of their legislative and constituent work. Committees are provided with staff assistance, subject to House or Senate approval of operating funds for each committee. Committees may also be given authority to hire temporary consultants (in addition to their full-time staff) or to accept assistance from staff of other government agencies loaned to the committees.

Each Chamber has an Office of Legislative Counsel to assist individual Members, committees, and staff in the drafting of legislation or in drafting amendments to bills, and both Houses maintain legislative libraries. Finally, each House has technical staff charged with providing computer services and automated systems services.

Additional support is provided by legislative branch agencies. The Congressional Research Service of the Library of Congress provides both committees and individual Members with information, research, and analysis on a wide range of subjects. The General Accounting Office assists committees and Members in fulfilling oversight and program evaluation responsibilities. The Congressional Budget Office provides specialized fiscal and budgetary analysis and cost estimates of Government agencies, programs, and operations.

45. Are there opportunities in the Congress to work as a volunteer, intern, or fellow?

Every year, large numbers of college students and other people work for Members of Congress as volunteers, as interns, or as fellows. Many colleges and universities award academic credit for congressional work, and a number of national professional associations sponsor a competitive, midcareer congressional fellowship appointment for interested organization members. The executive branch sponsors a Legis Fellows program, for midcareer Federal executives who wish to learn more about congressional operations. The officers of the House and Senate, along with several of the congressional support agencies, sponsor orientation programs for these congressional interns and fellows to acquaint them with congressional operations and with public policy research techniques.

46. Who are congressional pages? What are their duties and responsibilities? What facilities does Congress provide for them?

Congressional pages are boys and girls who are in their third year of high school, and assist members on the floor of the Chamber.

The page program in the House is supervised by the House Page Board and administered by the House Clerk. In the Senate, the party secretaries and the Sergeant at Arms have responsibility for the administration of the program.

The House and Senate each have schools for educating their pages. The House school is located in the Library of Congress and the Senate school is in the lower level of the Webster Residence Hall. The college preparatory curriculum includes additional programs, trips, and resources using facilities in Washington, DC.

Typically, the page schools meet during the mornings so that pages will be available for work during Chamber sessions later in the day.

CONGRESSIONAL PROCESS AND POWERS

47. Why must tax bills originate in the House?

The constitutional provision that "all Bills for raising Revenue shall originate in the House of Representatives" (Article I, Section 7) is an adaptation of an earlier English practice. It was based on the principle that the national purse strings should be controlled by a body directly responsible to the people. So when the Constitution was formulated, the authority for initiation of revenue legislation was vested in the House of Representatives where the Members are subject to direct election every two years. However, the Constitution also guarantees the Senate's power to "propose or concur with Amendments as on other Bills."

48. Must all appropriation measures originate in the House?

Although the Constitution clearly delegates sole authority to originate tax measures to the House of Representatives, it makes no clear statement regarding the authority to originate appropriation measures. Despite occasional disputes between the House and Senate over such authority, the House customarily originates general appropriation bills. The Senate from time to time initiates special appropriation measures that provide funds for a single agency or purpose.

49. What is the difference between an authorization and an appropriation?

Authorizations and appropriations are separate and distinct parts of the Federal budget process. Authorizations are measures which establish Federal policies and programs, and may also make recommendations concerning the proper spending level for a program or agency. Those recommendations are acted upon in the form of appropriations, which provide specific dollar amounts for agencies, programs, and operations. If an authorization specifies a spending level or upper limit, this amount acts as the maximum that an appropriation can provide. The rules of both the House and the Senate prohibit unauthorized appropriations, but both Chambers have developed practices to avoid the operation of these rules if it is the desire of the Chamber to do so.

50. What are the different types of appropriation measures?

Appropriations are provided in three different types of appropriation measures. Regular appropriation bills are a series of measures that together fund many Federal operations and programs for a fiscal year (October 1–September 30). Each of the 13 subcommittees of the House and Senate Appropriations Committees manages one regular appropriation bill. A supplemental appropriation bill is a measure which provides funds if a need develops that is too urgent to be postponed until the next fiscal year. Finally, a continuing resolution is a measure that provides stop-gap funding if Congress is unable to complete action on one or more regular appropriation bills before the beginning of a fiscal year.

All regular appropriation bills as well as supplemental appropriation bills that fund more than a single agency or purpose are also referred to as general appropriation bills.

51. What is the congressional budget process?

The congressional budget process, established by the Congressional Budget and Impoundment Control Act of 1974, is the means by which Congress develops and enforces an overall budgetary plan, including levels for total revenues, total spending, and a surplus or deficit. This blueprint for all Federal spending is established in the form of a concurrent resolution on the budget. Spending authority is then allocated to congressional committees pursuant to this resolution. The rules of both the House and Senate prohibit spending measures in excess of these allocations. Any changes in existing law that are necessary to achieve these targets can be enacted in the form of a reconciliation bill.

52. What is sequestration?

Sequestration is an across-the-board cut in Federal spending pursuant to a Presidential order. A sequestration order can only be issued if Congress fails to meet a budgetary requirement, such as a deficit target or a spending limit. Sequestration was first established in 1985 by the Balanced Budget and Emergency Deficit Reduction Act, also known as the Gramm-Rudman-Hollings Act.

53. What are the powers of Congress as provided in the Constitution?

The Constitution (Article 1, Section 8) empowers Congress to levy taxes, collect revenue, pay debts, and provide for the general welfare; borrow money; regulate interstate and foreign commerce; establish uniform rules of naturalization and bankruptcy; coin money and regulate its value; punish counterfeiters; establish a postal system; enact patent and copyright laws; establish Federal courts inferior to the Supreme Court; declare war; provide for the armed forces; impeach and try Federal officers (Sections 2 and 3); and have exclusive legislative power over the District of Columbia. In Article II, Section 2, the Senate is given the power to consent to the ratification of treaties and confirm the nomination of public officials. Congress is also given the power to enact such laws as may be "necessary and proper" to implement its mandate in Article I. The power to enact laws is also contained in certain amendments to the Constitution.

54. What is the confirmation power of the Senate?

Under Article II of the Constitution, the President appoints, by and with the advice and consent of the Senate, ambassadors, other public ministers and consuls, Justices of the Supreme Court and Federal judges, and other Federal officers whose appointments are established by law, including the heads of executive branch departments and agencies and independent regulatory commissions. This means that, while the President nominates the individuals of these important positions in the Federal Government, the Senate must confirm them before they take office. The Senate confirmation process can involve a background check of the nominee, often using information supplied by the Federal Bureau of Investigation; meetings between the nominee and individual Senators; hearings and a vote on the nomination by the committee with jurisdiction over the office; and debate and a vote in the full Senate, where a majority is necessary to confirm an appointment.

55. What is the role of Congress in the impeachment process?

Impeachment is the process by which the President, Vice President, Federal judges and Justices, and all civil officials of the United States may be removed from office. The President and other civil officials may be impeached and convicted for "Treason, Bribery, and other high Crimes and Misdemeanors."

The House of Representatives has the sole authority to bring charges of impeachment, by a simple majority vote, and the Senate has the sole authority to try impeachment charges. An official may be removed from office only upon conviction, which requires a two-thirds affirmative vote of the Senate. The Constitution provides that the Chief Justice shall preside when the President is being tried for impeachment.

56. Who controls use of the armed forces?

The Constitution (Article II, Section 2) states that the President is the Commander in Chief of the Army, Navy, and, when it is called into Federal service, State Militias (now called the National Guard). Historically, Presidents have used this authority to commit U.S. troops without a formal declaration of war. However, the Constitution reserves to Congress (Article I, Section 8) the power to raise and support the armed forces as well as the sole authority to declare war. These competing powers have been the source of controversy between the legislative and executive branches over war making. In 1973, Congress enacted the War Powers Resolution, which limits the President's authority to use the armed forces without specific congressional authorization, in an attempt to increase and clarify Congress's control over the use of the military. But the resolution has proven controversial, its operations has raised questions in Congress and the executive branch.

In addition, the armed forces operate under the doctrine of civilian control, which means that only the President or statutory deputies can order the use of force. The chain of command is structured to insure that the military cannot undertake actions without civilian approval or knowledge.

57. What is the procedure to commit the country's military force to war?

The Constitution gives to Congress the authority to declare war; this has occurred on only five occasions since 1789, the most recent being World War II. But the President, as Commander in Chief, has implied powers to commit the Nation's military forces, which has occurred on more than 200 occasions in U.S. history. Moreover, Congress may authorize the use of the military in specific cases through public law.

The War Powers Resolution, enacted on November 7, 1973, as Public Law 93–148, also tried to clarify these respective roles of the President and Congress in cases involving the use of armed forces without a declaration of war. The President is expected to consult with Congress before using the armed forces "in every possible instance," and is required to report to Congress within 48 hours of introducing troops. Use of the armed forces is to be terminated within 60 days, with a possible 30–day extension by the President, unless Congress acts during that time to declare war, enacts a specific authorization for use of the armed forces, extends the 60–90 day period, or is physically unable to meet as a result of an attack on the United States.

Congressional Rules and Procedures

58. How are the rules of procedure in Congress determined?

The Constitution (Article I, Section 5) provides that each House "determine the Rules of its Proceedings." These resulting rules and procedures are spelled out in detailed procedural manuals for each Chamber.

59. What are the functions of the House Rules Committee?

The House Rules Committee makes recommendations to the House on possible changes to the standing rules of the House, as well as the order of business on the House floor. The committee affects the order of business by reporting resolutions that make it possible for the House to begin acting on a bill that is on the House or Union Calendar. These resolutions are known as special rules or simply as "rules." Each special rule may also propose a set of ground rules for debating and amending a particular bill that is different from the normal rules for considering legislation. For example, a special rule may impose limitations on the amendments that Members can propose to a bill, or it may allow an amendment to be offered, even though it violates a standing rule of the House. The House as a whole decides by majority vote whether to accept, reject, or modify each special rule that the Rules Committee proposes.

The Senate Committee on Rules and Administration also considers possible changes to the standing rules of the Senate, but it has no role in determining the order of business on the Senate floor. In addition, the Senate committee reports resolutions to fund the work of all the Senate committees. In the House, this responsibility belongs to the Committee on House Administration.

60. What is a quorum of the House and of the Senate?

In the House of Representatives, a quorum is a simple majority of the Members. When there are no vacancies in the membership, a quorum is 218. When one or more seats are vacant, because of deaths or resignations, the quorum is reduced accordingly. Because of Members' other duties, a quorum often is not actually present on the House floor. If a Member makes a point of order that a quorum is not present, and the Speaker agrees, a series of bells ring on the House side of the Capitol and in the House office buildings to alert Members to come to the Chamber and record their presence.

A majority of the membership, or 51, constitutes a quorum to do business in the Senate.

61. What is the Committee of the Whole?

The Committee of the Whole House on the State of the Union (or Committee of the Whole) is a hybrid form of the House itself. Technically, it is a committee of the House on which all Representatives serve and that meets in the House Chamber. However, it is governed by different rules of procedure than the House meeting as itself. The concept of the "grand committee" has been carefully developed from the early days of the House and in modern practice gives the House a more expeditious means for considering the complex and often controversial legislation referred to it. Historically, it was devised by the English House of Commons to give them the ability to debate privately and not have their votes committed to record. The Committee of the Whole in the U.S. House permitted recorded votes beginning in January 1971.

The House resolves itself into a new Committee of the Whole for the consideration of each bill. A specific Committee of the Whole is dissolved when it "rises and reports with a recommendation," to the House. When the Committee rises after not having resolved the matter committed to it, that bill is carried on the calendar as "unfinished business of the Committee of the Whole" until consideration has been finally completed.

When a bill or resolution is considered in Committee of the Whole, there first is a period of time, usually one hour, for general debate on the merits of the bill or resolution. If enforced, a quorum in the Committee is 100 Members (whereas 218 are required in the House). After general debate, Members may offer amendments, with each speech for or against an amendment being limited to five minutes. If a recorded vote is desired on any amendment, the call for the vote must be seconded by 25 Members (whereas 44 or more are required in the House). When the amending process is completed, the Committee of the Whole "rises," and reports its actions to the House through the Speaker. The House then votes on whether or not to adopt the amendments recommended by the Committee of the Whole, and then votes on final passage of the measure, as amended.

The Senate ceased using the Committee of the Whole as a parliamentary forum for debate in 1986.

62. What are the duties of the Parliamentarians?

The House and the Senate each has a Parliamentarian to assist the Presiding Officer in making correct parliamentary decisions, to keep a record of procedures and precedents, and to refer bills to the correct committees of jurisdiction. These officials must be so well versed in the rules and practices of the Chamber that the Presiding Officer can be given guidance and advice on a moment's notice.

63. When Congress is in session, at what hour do the two Houses meet?

The time of meeting is fixed by each Chamber. However, the time at which House and Senate meetings begin or end is often changed from day to day, depending on the work that must be done.

64. What are the customary proceedings when the House of Representatives meets?

The Speaker calls the House to order, and the Sergeant at Arms places the Mace (an ancient symbol of authority) on the pedestal at the right of the Speaker's platform. After the Chaplain offers a prayer, the Speaker recognizes a Member to lead the House in the Pledge of Allegiance. Then the Journal of the previous day's activities is approved, usually without being read. Next, the Speaker may recognize a few Members to speak briefly on matters of importance to them, for no longer than one minute each. The House then is ready to begin or resume consideration of a bill, resolution, or conference report.

65. What are the customary proceedings when the Senate meets?

The initial proceedings of the Senate are similar. The Senate is called to order by the Vice President, the President pro tempore, or another Senator serving as acting President pro tempore. After a prayer, the pledge of allegiance and the approval of the Journal, the Majority and Minority Leaders are recognized in turn for brief periods to speak or to transact routine business. Other Senators then may speak, on matters of interest to them, for no longer than five minutes each. If the Senate had adjourned at the end of its previous meeting, a two-hour period, known as the "morning hour" is held, for disposing of routine and noncontroversial matters. If the Senate had recessed instead, which is the usual practice, there is no "morning hour" and the Senate proceeds instead to consider matters of legislative or executive business under its normal rules of procedure.

66. What business can be transacted by unanimous consent?

Almost anything can be done in either House by unanimous consent, except where the Constitution or the rules of that Chamber specifically prohibit the Presiding Officer from entertaining such a request. For example, since the Constitution requires that a rollcall vote be taken to pass a bill over a Presidential veto, the Presiding Officer of the House or the Senate cannot entertain a unanimous consent request to waive this requirement. In the House of Representatives, unanimous consent requests to admit to the Chamber persons who are not permitted to be present under its rules, or to introduce visitors in the galleries to the House, are not in order.

67. How are record votes taken in Congress?

Most votes are taken by a simple voice method, in which the yeas and nays are called out, respectively, and the judgment of the chair as to which are greater in number determines the vote. If a recorded vote is desired, a sufficient second must support it. The

Constitution simply provides that "the Yeas and Nays of the Members of either House on any question shall at the Desire of one-fifth of those present, be entered on the Journal." A sufficient second in the Committee of the Whole is 25. Since 1973, the House has used an electronic voting system to reduce the time consumed in voting. The Senate continues to use an oral call of the roll. Each Chamber permits a minimum of 15 minutes to complete a vote, though time for each vote may be reduced if several votes are conducted sequentially.

68. Are there time limitations on debate in Congress?

Yes. In the House, no matter is subject to more than one hour of debate, usually equally divided between the majority and the minority, without unanimous consent. Moreover, the majority can call for the "previous question," and bring the pending matter to an immediate vote. Nonlegislative debate is limited to one minute per Member at the beginning of the day and up to one hour per Member at the end of the day. In the Committee of the Whole, the period of time spent in general debate is determined and apportioned in advance. Amendments are subject to the five-minute per side rule, but can extend beyond 10 minutes of debate per amendment when unanimous consent is granted or when "pro forma" amendments are offered to gain additional time on the pending amendment. A nondebatable motion to close debate is in order to end debate on any specific amendment and bring it to a vote.

In the Senate, debate is normally without restriction, unless time limits are agreed to by unanimous consent. The ability to extend debate at will, to "filibuster," enables a Senator to delay the final vote on a measure, or even to prevent it altogether. Filibusters can be broken only by negotiation or through the use of a formal procedure known as "cloture." A successful cloture motion requires at least a 3/5 vote, or 60 Senators. If cloture is invoked, the filibuster comes to a gradual end. Thirty hours of further debate are permitted in the post-cloture period prior to the vote on final passage. However, Senators do not usually extend debate after a successful cloture vote.

69. How do Members obtain permission to speak?

In the House, Members stand, address the Presiding Officer and do not proceed until recognized to speak. The Presiding Officer (the Speaker in the House or the Chairman in the Committee of the Whole) has the authority to ask Members for what purpose they seek recognition. The Presiding Officer may then recognize or not recognize a Member, depending upon the purpose for which recognition was requested.

In the Senate, Senators must also stand, address the Presiding Officer (the Vice President, the President pro tempore, or the acting President pro tempore), and may not proceed until one of them is recognized to speak. However, the rules of the Senate require the Presiding Officer to recognize the first Senator to address the chair. The Presiding Officer does not have discretionary recognition authority. However, in the tradition of the Senate, the Majority Leader and Minority Leader are given preferential recognition over any other Senator.

70. How do Members of Congress introduce bills?

A bill that is to be introduced is typed on a special House or Senate form and signed by the Representative or Senator who will introduce it. In the House, a Representative may introduce a bill any time the House is in session by placing it in a special box known as the "hopper," which is located on the Clerk's desk in the House Chamber. A Senator introduces a bill by delivering it to a clerk on the Senate floor while the Senate is in session, although it is formally accepted only during a period of time set aside in the Senate for the transacting of routine morning business.

71. When does a bill, introduced at the beginning of a Congress, become "dead" and no longer open to considerations?

A bill may be introduced at any point during a two-year Congress, and remains eligible for consideration throughout the duration of that Congress until the Congress ends or adjourns sine die.

72. What are the stages of a bill in Congress?

Following is a brief description of the usual stages by which a bill becomes law. (A graphic follows this explanation that illustrates these stages, How a Bill Becomes a Law.)

(1) Introduction by a Member, who places it in the "hopper," a box on the Clerk's desk in the House Chamber; the bill is given a number and printed by the Government Printing Office so that copies are available the next morning.

(2) Referral to one or more standing committees of the House by the Speaker, at the advice of the Parliamentarian.

(3) Report from the committee or committees, after public hearings and "markup" meetings by subcommittee, committee, or both.

(4) House approval of a special rule, reported by the House Rules Committee, making it in order for the House to consider the bill, and setting the terms for its debate and amendment.

(5) Consideration of the bill in Committee of the Whole, in two stages: first, a time for general debate on the bill; and second, a time for amending the bill, one part at a time, under a rule that limits speeches on amendments to five minutes each.

(6) Passage by the House after votes to confirm the amendments that were adopted in Committee of the Whole.

(7) Transmittal to the Senate, by message.

(8) Consideration and passage by the Senate—usually after referral to and reporting from a Senate committee—and after debate and amendment on the Senate floor.

(9) Transmission from the Senate back to the House, with or without Senate amendments to the bill.

(10) Resolution of differences between the House and the Senate, either through additional amendments between the Houses, or the report of a conference committee.

(11) Enrollment on parchment paper and then signing by the Speaker and by the President of the Senate.

(12) Transmittal to the President of the United States.

(13) Approval or disapproval by the President; if the President disapproves, the bill will be returned with a veto message that explains reasons for the disapproval. A two-thirds vote in each chamber is needed to override a veto.

(14) Filing with the Archivist of the United States as a new public law after approval of the President, or after passage by Congress overriding a veto.

Bills may be introduced in the Senate, and they follow essentially the same course of passage as bills first introduced and considered in the House of Representatives. (See questions above, however, on the House originating tax and appropriations bills.)

75. How does a bill become law?

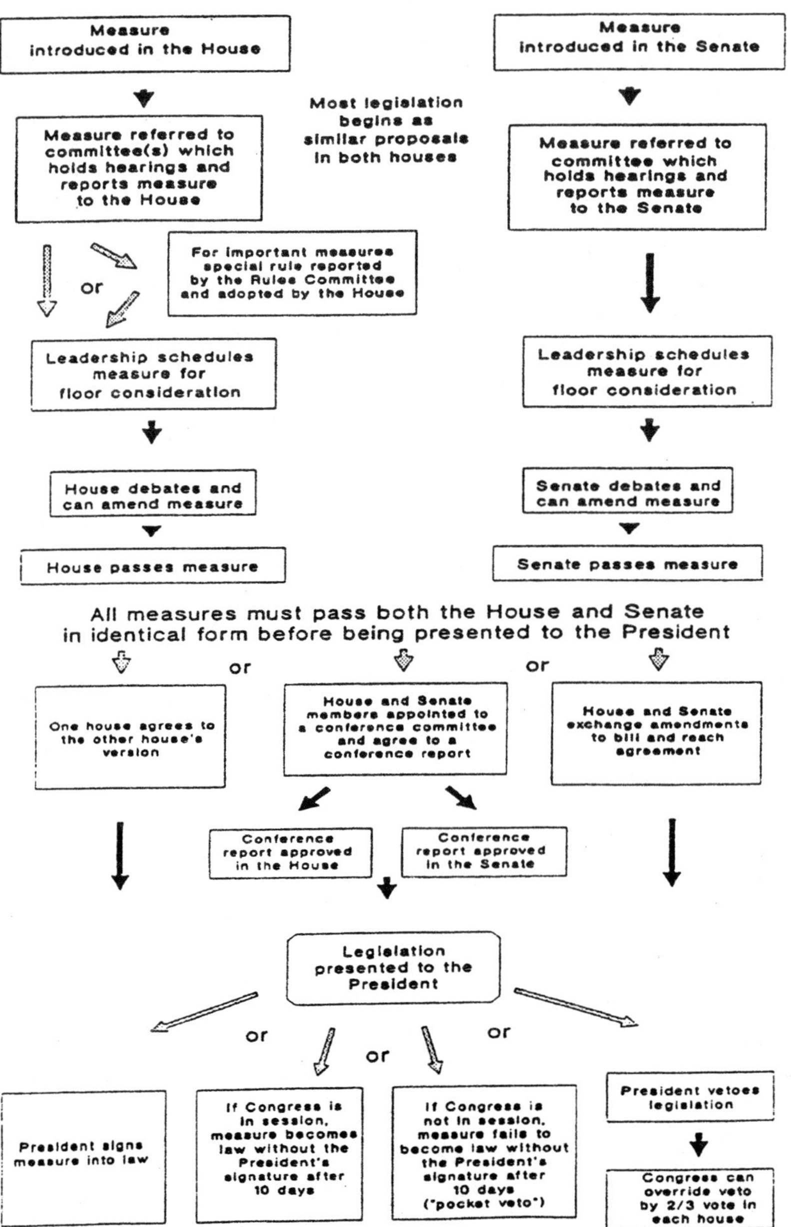

73. What courses are open to the President when a bill is presented to him?

The President has three choices: First, to sign a bill within 10 days (Sundays excepted), whereupon it becomes a law. Second, the President may veto the bill, i.e., return it to Congress (stating objections) without a signature of approval. In this case, Congress may override the veto with a two-thirds vote in each House. The bill would then become a law despite the President's veto. The House and Senate are not required to attempt veto overrides. Third, the President may hold the bill without taking any action. Two different developments may occur in this situation depending upon whether Congress is in session. If Congress is in session, the bill becomes law after the expiration of 10 days (excluding Sundays), even without the President's signature. If Congress has adjourned at the end of a Congress the bill does not become law; this is called a "pocket veto".

74. What happens to a bill after it becomes law?

The provisions of a law take effect immediately unless the law itself provides for another date. The law may also specify which executive departments, agencies, or officers are empowered to carry out or enforce the law.

The actual written document is sent to the National Archives and Records Administration, an independent agency of the Government, where it is given a number. It is then published in individual form as a "slip law." At the end of each session of Congress, these new laws are consolidated in a bound volume called U.S. Statutes at Large. In addition, all permanent, general laws currently in force are included in the Code of Laws of the United States of America, commonly called the U.S. Code. The Office of Law Revision Counsel, part of the institutional structure of the House of Representatives, is responsible for preparing and issuing annual supplements to keep the Code up-to-date.

75. Are the proceedings of Congress published and preserved?

Each House, by constitutional requirement, keeps a Journal of its proceedings. The Senate maintains and publishes a legislative journal and an executive journal. The latter contains proceedings related to the Senate's responsibilities for approving treaties and nominations. When the Senate sits as a court of impeachment, it keeps a separate journal of its proceedings. The executive journal is published annually.

The Journals do not report debates; they only report the bare parliamentary proceedings of each Chamber. In addition, the House Journal contains minimal information about actions taken by the House when meeting as a Committee of the Whole, because any action taken there is not official unless and until it is ratified by the full House.

For a public record of the debates, there have been a succession of reports, overlapping in part, as follows: Annals of Congress (1789–1824), Register of Debates (1824–37), Congressional Globe

(1833–73), and finally and currently the Congressional Record (1873 to the present).

The Congressional Record contains a stenographic record of everything said on the floor of both Houses, including rollcall votes on all questions. Members are permitted to edit and revise the transcripts of their spoken remarks. An appendix contains material not spoken on the floor but inserted by permission—the so-called "extensions of remarks." It also carries a brief resume of the congressional activities of the previous day, as well as a future legislative program and a list of scheduled committee hearings.

Since 1979 in the House and 1986 in the Senate, floor sessions have been televised. Videotape copies of House and Senate Chamber activities are preserved and available for research use at the Library of Congress and at the National Archives.

76. What are joint sessions and joint meetings?

Congress holds joint sessions to receive addresses from the President (e.g., State of the Union and other addresses) and to count electoral ballots for President and Vice President. Congress also holds joint meetings to receive addresses from such dignitaries as foreign heads of state or heads of governments or from distinguished American citizens.

Of the two types of gatherings, the joint session is the more formal and typically occurs upon adoption of a concurrent resolution passed by both Houses of Congress. The joint meeting, however, typically occurs when each of the two Houses adopts a unanimous consent agreement to recess to meet with the other legislative body. Since 1809, the prevailing practice has been to hold joint sessions and joint meetings in the Hall of the House of Representatives, the larger of the two Chambers.

Except for the first inauguration in 1789, in which the Congress convened in joint session to inaugurate President George Washington, these special occasions have occurred outside of the regular legislative calendars. Occasionally one chamber will convene a legislative session prior to attending the ceremony, but unless both do so and subsequently adjourn to attend the ceremony, the inauguration is not a joint session.

77. May the Secretary of State or any other Cabinet officer appear on the floor of either House to answer questions?

No. Cabinet officers frequently testify before House and Senate committees and subcommittees, but they may not appear on the floor of either Chamber to respond publicly to Members' questions. There have been proposals to permit such a "question period" by amending congressional rules, but they have not been approved.

78. Are visitors allowed to listen to the proceedings of Congress?

Visitors are allowed to listen to and watch the proceedings of the House and Senate from visitors' galleries in each House. Tour guides bring groups of visitors briefly into the House and Senate galleries. Visitors who wish to observe House and Senate floor sessions for longer periods of time without interruption must obtain gallery passes, available without prior notice in the offices of their Senator or Representative.

All visitors must abide by certain rules and maintain proper decorum. They are not allowed to take radios, cameras, or umbrellas into either Chamber and they may not read, write, or take notes while inside. Visitors in the galleries are subject to control and supervision by the Presiding Officers of the House and Senate as well as doorkeepers stationed beside each entrance to the galleries. Unless there is a rare closed meeting of either House, visitors are allowed whenever Congress is in session.

Most committee hearings and meetings are also open to the public. Committees generally meet in rooms set aside for their use in the congressional office buildings and no visitors' passes are required, although audience space may be limited to accommodate congressional staff, executive branch officials, and journalists. Under certain circumstances specified in House and Senate Rules, committees may vote to close hearings or meetings to the public.

Special space is available in the galleries for accredited journalists, who are not subject to the prohibition on writing and taking notes. Since 1979, proceedings of the House have been accessible to the news media for television or radio broadcast. Senate sessions have been available for television and radio broadcast since 1986. Any committee hearing or meeting open to the public can also be broadcast on radio or television, subject to administrative control by the individual committee.

THE COMMITTEE SYSTEM

79. Has Congress ever altered its committee organization?

Congressional organization and procedure have changed considerably over Congress's 200-year history in response to new needs and circumstances.

With respect to the committee system, for example, in the early years of the Republic, Congress relied on temporary, ad hoc committees to process legislation the full Chambers had considered. A system of permanent standing committees developed in the first half of the 19th century, when committees acquired many modern-day powers, such as the power to hold legislation they do not recommend for full Chamber action. Throughout the 19th century, so many committees were created to deal with emerging national issues that, by the 20th century, the system had become unwieldy. Early 20th century action by the Chambers abolished and consolidated panels to streamline decision making.

Major reorganization of the committee system was also achieved by the Legislative Reorganization Act of 1946. It established standardized committee procedures in many areas, abolished and merged committees to form integrated panels with broad jurisdictions, and gave each standing committee a permanent complement of staff. The act also revamped other areas of congressional procedure. For example, it established the first comprehensive laws to regulate the lobbying of Congress, which have since been amended. A similar 1970 Reorganization Act revised committee and other procedures, including strengthening Congress's fiscal controls. A

1974 House committee reform measure refined committees' jurisdictions, amended committee procedures, and expanded Congress's oversight of the executive branch. A 1977 Senate committee reform measure realigned and consolidated jurisdictions, revised and expanded Senators' service limitations on committees, and amended procedures for hiring staff and referring legislation, among other things. In 1993, another reform review was initiated by the Joint Committee on the Organization of Congress.

80. What is a conference committee?

From the earliest days, differences on legislation between the House and Senate have been committed to conference committees to work out a settlement. The most usual case is that in which a bill passes one Chamber with amendments unacceptable to the other. In such a case, the Chamber that disagrees to the amendments generally asks for a conference, and the Speaker of the House and the Presiding Officer of the Senate appoint the "managers," as the conferees are called. Generally, they are selected from the committee or committees having charge of the bill. After attempting to resolve the points in disagreement, the conference committee issues a report to each Chamber. If the report is accepted by both Chambers, the bill is then enrolled and sent to the President. If the report is rejected by either Chamber, the matter in disagreement comes up for disposition anew as if there had been no conference. Unless all differences between the two Houses are resolved, the bill fails.

Until 1975, it was customary for conference committees to meet in executive sessions closed to the public. In that year, both chambers adopted rules to require open conference meetings. Two years later, the House strengthened its open conference rule. Today, most conference committee sessions are open to public observation, with only a few exceptions for national security, or for other reasons.

81. What are congressional standing committees and why are they necessary?

Standing committees are permanent panels comprised of Members of a Chamber. Each panel has jurisdiction over measures and laws in certain areas of public policy, such as health, education, energy, the environment, foreign affairs, and agriculture.

Although Congress has used standing committees since its earliest days, it did not predominantly rely on them during its first quarter century. In these early years, legislative proposals were considered initially by all Members of one Chamber in plenary session; afterwards, each proposal was referred to a temporary, ad hoc committee responsible for working out a proposal's details and making any technical changes. As the amount of legislative proposals increased, especially in certain subject areas, permanent committees replaced temporary ones for more expeditious screening and processing of legislation before its consideration by an entire Chamber.

Each Chamber now has its own standing committees, to allow it to consider many issues at the same time. Each committee selects, from the measures it receives each Congress, a relatively small number that merit committee scrutiny and subsequent consideration by the full Chamber. Because of the small size of committees—and the often lengthy service of Members on the same panel—committees provide an effective means of managing Congress's enormous workload and gaining expertise over the range and complexity of subjects with which the Government deals.

82. What are the standing committees of the House?

In 2003, the 19 standing committees were named: Agriculture; Appropriations; Armed Services; Budget; Education and the Workforce; Energy and Commerce; Financial Services; Government Reform; House Administration; International Relations; Judiciary; Resources; Rules; Science; Small Business; Standards of Official Conduct; Transportation and Infrastructure; Veterans' Affairs; and Ways and Means.

83. What are the standing committees of the Senate?

In 2003, 16 standing committees were named: Agriculture, Nutrition, and Forestry; Appropriations; Armed Services; Banking, Housing, and Urban Affairs; Budget; Commerce, Science, and Transportation; Energy and Natural Resources; Environment and Public Works; Finance; Foreign Relations; Governmental Affairs; Health, Education, Labor, and Pensions; Judiciary; Rules and Administration; Small Business and Entrepreneurship; and Veterans' Affairs.

84. How are the members of the standing committees selected?

Before Members are assigned to committees, each committee's size and the proportion of Democrats to Republicans must be decided by each Chamber's party leaders. The total number of committee slots allotted to each party is approximately the same as the ratio between majority-party and minority-party Members in the full Chamber. Members are then assigned to committees in a three-step process, where the first is the most critical and decisive. Each of the two principal parties in the House and Senate is responsible for assigning its Members to committees, and, at the first stage, each party uses a committee on committees to make the initial recommendations for assignments. At the beginning of a new Congress, Members express preferences for assignment to the appropriate committee on committees; most incumbents prefer to remain on the same committees so as not to forfeit expertise and committee seniority. These committees on committees then match preferences with committee slots, following certain guidelines designed in part to distribute assignments fairly. They then prepare and approve an assignment slate for each committee, and submit all slates to the appropriate full-party conference for approval. Approval at this second stage often is granted easily, but the conferences have procedures for disapproving recommended Members and nominating others in their stead. Finally, at the third stage, each committee submits its slate to the pertinent full Chamber for approval, which is generally granted readily.

85. What constitutes a quorum of a standing committee of the House and of the Senate?

Each House and Senate committee is authorized to establish its own quorum requirement for the transaction of business. House rules specify that House committees shall have at least two members present to take testimony or receive evidence and at least one third of the members present for taking any other action, except reporting out a bill to the floor. Senate rules also require at least one-third of the committee membership present to conduct most business, but permit committees to lower that quorum requirement for purposes of taking testimony. However, in both Chambers, a physical majority of the committee members must be present to report a bill to the floor.

86. What is a select committee?

In the contemporary era, select committees are established by the House and Senate usually for limited time periods and for strictly limited purposes. In most cases, they have not been accorded legislative power—the authority to consider and report legislation to the full Chamber. After completing their purpose, such as an investigation of a Government activity and making a report thereon, the select committee expires. Recently, however, the Chambers have permitted select committees to continue to exist over long periods; some, such as the House and Senate Select Committees on Intelligence, have been granted legislative authority.

87. What are joint committees and how are they established?

Joint committees are those that have Members chosen from both the House and Senate, generally with the chairmanship rotating between the most senior majority-party Senator and Representative. In general, they do not have legislative power to consider and report legislation to the full Chambers. These committees can be created by statute, or by joint or concurrent resolution, although all existing ones have been established by statute. Congress now has four permanent or long-term joint committees, the oldest being the Joint Committee on the Library, which dates from 1800; the other three are the Joint Economic Committee, Joint Committee on Printing, and Joint Committee on Taxation. In addition, Congress sometimes establishes temporary joint committees for particular purposes, such as the Joint Congressional Committee on Inaugural Ceremonies, which is formed every four years to handle the organizational and financial responsibilities for the inauguration of the President and Vice President.

88. Do congressional committees hold hearings on all bills referred to them?

No. There may also be several bills similar or almost identical in substance introduced at the same time. In such cases, hearings frequently are held on a group of related measures, or a hearing on one bill serves for all similar bills. It is not always possible for Members to have individual hearings on their particular bills before a committee because of the press of business and the large number of bills referred to most committees.

89. Does the congressional committee to which a bill is referred effectively control its disposition?

Committees, for the most part, control whether hearings will be held on bills referred to them and whether these bills will be reported to the full Chamber for debate. Ordinarily, if a bill is not reported by a committee, the bill dies because the Chambers usually defer to the expertise and power of committee members in determining a measure's fate.

However, both the House and Senate have procedures for allowing measures not reported by a committee to be considered by the full Chamber. The House has a discharge procedure, usually used with measures of a controversial character. It is rarely employed and rarely successful, because it is cumbersome and because Members are uncomfortable circumventing committee authority. The procedure allows a majority of Representatives (218) to sign a petition to discharge a committee of any bill held there longer than 30 days, at which point the bill is placed on a special calendar and may be called up by any of the signers on the second or fourth Monday of any month. Very limited debate is allowed on the question of whether to consider a bill on the calendar. But, if the House agrees by majority to a bill's consideration, then it is debated under its general rules.

It is also possible to discharge a Senate committee by motion, but the procedure is rarely used. Instead, because the Senate does not generally require amendments to measures to be on the same subject as the measures, a Senator may offer the text of a measure buried in committee as an amendment to any measure being debated by the full Senate. This practice is not allowed in the House, where amendments must be relevant (called "germane") to the measures they seek to amend.

90. Are committee hearings open to the public?

Hearings by House committees and subcommittees are open to the public except when a committee, by majority vote while in public session, determines otherwise. This occurs, for instance, when national security matters are considered.

The Legislative Reorganization Act of 1970 permitted, for the first time, radio and television broadcast of House committee and subcommittee hearings.

Hearings by Senate committees and subcommittees are also open to the public. However, Senate committee hearings may be closed to the public if the committee determines by majority vote in open session that testimony must be secret for any of several reasons, including if it relates to national security matters, reflects adversely on the character or reputation of witnesses, or divulges information which is of a confidential nature.

Hearings of public interest in the Senate have been broadcast for more than 40 years.

91. What is meant by the "seniority rule"?

It had been the custom whereby a member who served longest on the majority side of a committee became its chairman or if on the minority, its ranking member. Members were ranked from the chairman or ranking member down, according to length of service on the committee.

Modifications—including party practices, term limits on chairmanships, and limits on the number of committees and subcommittees chaired—have caused the seniority rule to be less rigidly followed than previously. Nevertheless, length of service on a committee remains the predominant criterion for choosing its chairman and ranking member. In both Chambers, nominees for committee chairmen are subject to public votes, first in meetings of their party colleagues (in conference or caucus), then in the full Chamber. Members who interrupt their service in a Chamber but subsequently return to the Congress, start again at the bottom of a committee list. Returning Members outrank other new Members who have no prior service. New Members also earn seniority over other newly elected Members by having prior service in the other legislative Chamber. In some cases, in which two Members have equal time in service in a Chamber, prior service as a State Governor or State legislator also may contribute in the determination of seniority.

THE EXECUTIVE BRANCH

92. How is the executive branch organized?

The Federal executive branch is headed by the President and consists of various entities and organizations of largely an administrative, regulatory, or policy-implementing character. Most prominent among these are 15 departments, whose heads comprise the Cabinet. In addition, there are a number of agencies (such as the Central Intelligence Agency and Environmental Protection Agency) plus separate smaller boards, committees, commissions, and offices created by law or Presidential directive. Immediately assisting the President are the agencies and entities of the Executive Office of the President. Additional information on the White House and Presidential activities is at <www.whitehouse.gov>.

93. What is the Executive Office of the President?

Formally established in 1939, the Executive Office of the President consists of satellite offices and agencies that assist the President in the exercise of various statutory responsibilities. Later, as conditions merited, such units were abolished or transferred to program departments and agencies of the executive branch. (See accompanying graphic, White House and Executive Office of the President.)

White House and Executive Office of the President

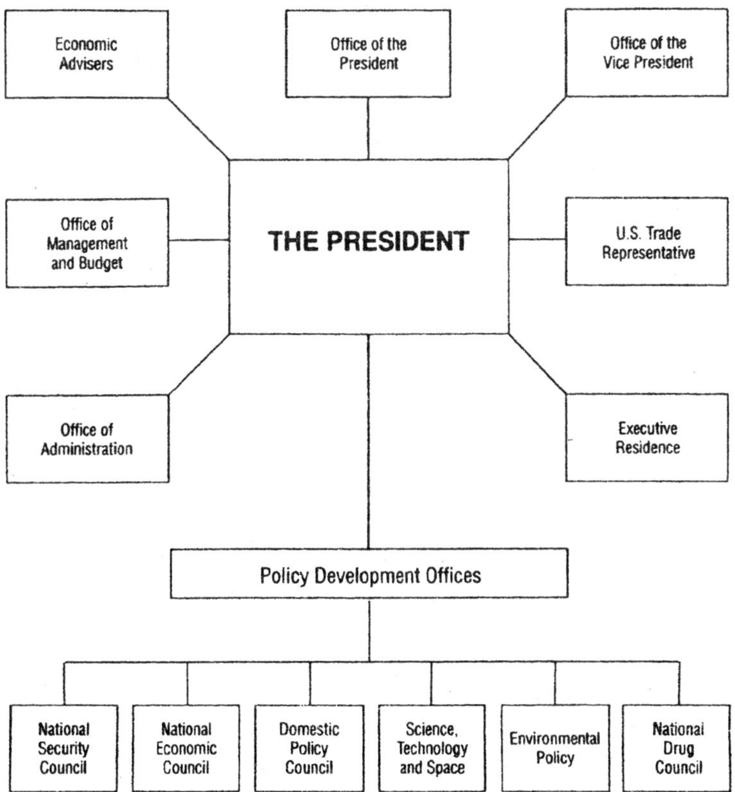

WHITE HOUSE AND EXECUTIVE OFFICE OF THE PRESIDENT

THE PRESIDENT AND VICE PRESIDENT

94. Is the U.S. President comparable to a reigning monarch, a prime minister, or a premier?

The American President has been compared to an elective monarch, but there are few kings or queens today who exercise the same degree of authority as does the President of the United States. The President simultaneously serves to perform functions that parallel the activities of a king or queen in a monarchy and the prime minister or premier in a parliamentary democracy.

The President is traditionally accorded the unofficial designation "Chief of State," a position which most closely parallels that of a king or queen in a monarchy. As such the President is often recognized as the symbolic embodiment of the United States and its citizens.

The President also performs many of the functions of a prime minister or premier in a parliamentary democracy. As Chief Executive, an office held under the Constitution, the President presides over the Cabinet and has responsibility for the management of the executive branch. The Constitution also vests the President with the power to make treaties, and to appoint ambassadors, U.S. officers, and judges of Federal courts, with the advice and consent of the Senate. The President also holds the position of Commander in Chief of the Armed Forces.

Unlike a prime minister, the President is neither a member of the legislature nor is his tenure in office dependent upon the approval of a majority of legislators. Elected indirectly by the citizens through the electoral college, the President serves a definite term and can only be removed by the process of impeachment. Under the 22nd Amendment, presidential tenure is limited to no more than two elected four-year terms and a maximum of 10 years under special circumstances: i.e., if a twice-elected President serves an additional two years (or less) of the term of another elected President.

95. How is the President addressed?

Simply as "Mr. President." A letter sent to the Chief Executive is addressed "The President, The White House."

One of the earliest congressional debates dealt with the title of the Chief Executive. A committee of the House of Representatives suggested the simple title "The President of the United States." However, the Senate rejected this report in May 1789 at the behest of Vice President John Adams. Adams believed that "titles and politically inspired elegance were essential aspects of strong government," and supported the title "His Highness the President of the United States and protector of their Liberties." George Washington himself was annoyed by this debate and made known his annoyance at Adams's attempts to "bedizen him with a superb but spurious title." The issue was resolved on May 27 when the Senate agreed that the Chief Executive should have the simple title "the President of the United States."

96. What are the enumerated or express constitutional powers of the President?

Article II of the Constitution vests the "executive power" in the President. There is dispute among scholars as to whether such executive power consists solely of the authorities enumerated for the President or whether it also includes powers that are implied in Article II. Most authorities lean toward the latter interpretation.

These powers are those expressly granted to the President within the text of the Constitution. They are few in number and most are listed in Article II, sections 2 and 3 of the Constitution. The President is Commander in Chief of the Army, Navy, and Air Force, and of the State Militias (now called the National Guard) when called into the service of the United States. The President may require the written opinion of military executive officers, and is empowered to grant reprieves and pardons, except in the case of impeachment. The President receives ambassadors and other public ministers, ensures that the laws are faithfully executed, and commissions all officers of the United States. The President has power, by and with the advice and consent of the Senate, to make treaties, provided that two-thirds of the Senators present concur. The President also nominates and appoints ambassadors, other public ministers and consuls, Justices of the Supreme Court, Federal judges, and other Federal officers whose appointments are established by law, by and with the advice and consent of the Senate. The President has the power to fill temporarily all vacancies that occur during the recess of the Senate. Also, the President may, on extraordinary occasions, convene "emergency" sessions of Congress. Furthermore, if the two Houses disagree as to the time of adjournment, the President himself may adjourn the bodies. In addition to these powers, the President also has enumerated powers that allow him to directly influence legislation. The Constitution directs the President periodically to inform Congress on the State of the Union, and to recommend legislation that is considered necessary and expedient. Also, in Article I, section 7, the Constitution grants the President the authority to veto acts of Congress.

97. What are the implied constitutional powers of the President?

In addition to express powers, the President possesses powers that are not enumerated within the Constitution's text. These implied powers have been, and continue to be, a subject of dispute and debate. The task of attributing implied powers to the President is complicated by three factors: the importance of the presidency in the political strategy of the Constitution; the President's extensive and vaguely defined authority in international relations; and the fact that the President is often said to have inherent or residual powers of authority.

For example, although the Constitution does not grant to the President express power to remove administrators from their offices, as the chief executive, the President holds power over executive branch officers, unless such removal power is limited by public law. The President, however, does not have such implied authority over officers in independent establishments. When President

Franklin D. Roosevelt removed a member of the Federal Trade Commission, an independent regulatory agency, and not part of the executive branch, the Supreme Court, in 1935, ruled the removal invalid.

Another implied constitutional power is derived from the President's authority as Commander in Chief. Though the Congress has the explicit power to declare war, the President not only has the responsibility to protect the Nation from sudden attack, but also has initiated military activities abroad without a formal declaration of war. American Presidents have authorized military force abroad more than 225 times, but only on five occasions has Congress declared war: The War of 1812, the Mexican War, the Spanish-American War, World War I, and World War II. In recent years, most notably through the War Powers Resolution of 1973, Congress has sought to define more clearly the conditions under which Presidents unilaterally can authorize military action abroad.

98. It is constitutionally mandated that the President is Commander in Chief of the Army and the Navy. What about the other military services?

Organizationally, the U.S. Marine Corps is a part of the U.S. Navy, and the military service that is now the U.S. Air Force was once part of the U.S. Army. These four military services are a part of the Department of Defense, an executive branch department. Congress, moreover, has provided that, subject to the direction of the President and applicable laws, the Secretary of Defense has authority, direction, and control over the Department of Defense and, thus, over the Armed Forces. During time of war or as directed by the President, the commissioned corps of the Public Health Service may be declared to be a military service by Executive order. Likewise, the Coast Guard, usually a part of the U.S. Department of Transportation, operates as part of the U.S. Navy in time of war or when directed by the President.

99. What is a Presidential veto?

There are two types of vetoes available to the President. One, the regular veto, is a "qualified negative veto," which is limited by the ability of Congress to muster the necessary two-thirds vote of each House for constitutional override. The other type of veto is not explicitly designated in the U.S. Constitution but is traditionally called a "pocket veto." This veto is actually an "absolute veto" that cannot be overridden. It becomes effective when the President fails to sign a bill after Congress has adjourned and is unable to override the veto.

The President's veto authority is one of the significant tools in legislative dealings with Congress. It is not only effective in directly preventing the passage of legislation undesirable to the President, but also as a threat, thereby bringing about changes in the content of legislation long before the bill is ever presented to the President.

100. Have many bills been vetoed by Presidents?

As of August 31, 2003, U.S. Presidents have vetoed 2,550 bills presented to them by Congress. Of that total number, 1,484 were regular vetoes, and 1,066 were pocket vetoes. This may appear to be a large number of vetoes, but it actually represents about 3 percent of the approximately 93,555 bills presented to U.S. Presidents since George Washington. (See the accompanying table, Vetoes by Presidents.)

VETOES BY PRESIDENTS

[Through August 31, 2003]

President	Regular vetoes	Pocket vetoes	Total vetoes	Vetoes over-ridden
George Washington	2	....	2	....
John Adams	....	....	0	....
Thomas Jefferson	....	....	0	....
James Madison	5	2	7	....
James Monroe	1	....	1	....
John Quincy Adams	....	....	0	....
Andrew Jackson	5	7	12	....
Martin Van Buren	....	1	1	....
William Henry Harrison	....	....	0	....
John Tyler	6	4	10	1
James K. Polk	2	1	3	....
Zachary Taylor	....	....	0	....
Millard Fillmore	....	....	0	....
Franklin Pierce	9	....	9	5
James Buchanan	4	3	7	....
Abraham Lincoln	2	5	7	....
Andrew Johnson	21	8	29	15
Ulysses S. Grant	45	48	93	4
Rutherford B. Hayes	12	1	13	1
James A. Garfield	....	....	0	....
Chester A. Arthur	4	8	12	1
Grover Cleveland (1st term)	304	110	414	2
Benjamin Harrison	19	25	44	1
Grover Cleveland (2nd term)	42	128	170	5
William McKinley	6	36	42	....
Theodore Roosevelt	42	40	82	1
William H. Taft	30	9	39	1
Woodrow Wilson	33	11	44	6
Warren G. Harding	5	1	6	....
Calvin Coolidge	20	30	50	4
Herbert C. Hoover	21	16	37	3
Franklin D. Roosevelt	372	263	635	9
Harry S Truman	180	70	250	12
Dwight D. Eisenhower	73	108	181	2
John F. Kennedy	12	9	21	....
Lyndon B. Johnson	16	14	30	....
Richard M. Nixon	26	17	43	7
Gerald R. Ford	48	18	66	12
James E. Carter	13	18	31	2
Ronald W. Reagan	39	39	78	9
George H.W. Bush	29	[1] 15	44	1
William J. Clinton	36	1	37	2
George W. Bush	0	0	0	0
Total	1,484	1,066	2,550	106

[1] President Bush asserted that two bills were not enacted into law under the pocket veto provisions of the Constitution because Congress was in recess. Congress, however, maintained that these were not vetoes because they required action within 10 days of receipt by the President; both ultimately were considered to be law. A third bill was asserted by President Bush to be pocket-vetoed during a congressional recess, but he returned a veto message to the originating House and it was treated as a regular veto. For further explanation, See U.S. Congress, Office of the Secretary of the Senate, Presidential Vetoes, 1989–1996, S. Pub. 105–22 (Washington: GPO, September 1997), pp. 6, 12.

101. Are acts often passed over the President's veto?

This occurs very rarely, because pocket vetoes cannot be overridden and regular vetoes require a two-thirds vote in each House of Congress. As a consequence, regular vetoes have been overridden by Congress only 106 times in over 200 years. Presidents may also be anxious about a poor public image resulting from having a veto overridden by Congress and, depending on the circumstances, may be hesitant to use it unless reasonably assured of being sustained.

The U.S. President with the highest percentage of veto overrides was Andrew Johnson (71.4 percent), followed by Presidents Pierce (55.5 percent), Nixon (26.9 percent), Ford (25.0 percent), Arthur (25.0 percent), and Reagan (22.9 percent).

102. What important court cases relate to the pocket veto?

In practice, Presidents have found the pocket veto to be a useful tool and have employed it frequently (42.5 percent of all vetoes), both because Congress has adjourned and because it precludes a potential override by Congress. Supporters of congressional prerogatives, on the other hand, object to unconstitutional use (in their view) of the pocket veto, because, as an absolute veto, it diminishes the capacity of Congress to function as a coequal branch of Government in legislative matters.

Attempts in Federal courts to determine the limits of the pocket veto have satisfied neither the executive nor the legislative branch of Government. Federal court opinions have sustained the President's use of the pocket veto at the end of a complete congressional cycle. What remains in contention, despite various court rulings and agreements with two administrations, is whether the President can pocket veto a bill between the first and second sessions of a Congress or during intrasession adjournments of more than 3 days.

The Supreme Court has ruled in only two cases related to the pocket veto issue. The *Pocket Veto Case*, 279 U.S. 644 (1929), is probably the most famous of the rulings. In this case, the Supreme Court ruled that the President may pocket veto a measure not only after the final adjournment of a Congress, but also during the adjournment after the first session. According to the Court, the intersession adjournment prevented the President (Coolidge) from returning the bill, and the measure did not become law.

The second Supreme Court opinion came in *Wright* v. *United States*, 302 U.S. 583 (1938). The Supreme Court held in *Wright* that the bill in question had been properly returned to the Senate by the President and, in the absence of a congressional vote to override, it could not become law. In contrast to the views it had expressed in the *Pocket Veto Case*, the *Wright* opinion approved the President's return of a vetoed bill to an agent (official of the Senate) of the originating House, even though that body was not in session.

Lower court opinions have also affected the use of the pocket veto. In 1974, the U.S. Court of Appeals for the District of Columbia Circuit extended the decision in *Wright* by ruling that an intrasession adjournment of Congress does not prevent the President from returning a bill to Congress so long as appropriate arrangements are made for the receipt of veto message during an adjournment, *Kennedy* v. *Sampson*, 511 F.2d 430 (D.C. Cir. 1974).

In other litigation, two 1974 pocket vetoes, one by President Richard Nixon during a 29-day intersession adjournment and one by President Gerald Ford during a 31-day intrasesession adjournment, were contested in court. These pocket vetoes were invalidated when the Justice Department agreed to the summary judgment in *Kennedy* v. *Jones*, 412 F. Supp. 353, 356 (D.D.C. 1976).

In *Barnes* v. *Carmen*, 582 F. Supp. 163 (D.D.C. 1984), a pocket veto by President Ronald Reagan between sessions of the 98th Congress was upheld by the district court, following the ruling in the *Pocket Veto Case*. In a 2-to-1 decision in *Barnes* v. *Kline*, 759 F.2d 21 (D.C. Cir. 1985), the Court of Appeals for the District of Columbia Circuit found that use of the pocket veto during an intersession adjournment to be unconstitutional, and rested the decision on the reasoning in *Wright* and *Kennedy* v. *Sampson*. That decision was vacated as moot by the Supreme Court in *Burke* v. *Barnes*, 479 U.S. 361 (1987). The Supreme Court did not reach the pocket veto issue since the bill in question (H.R. 4042, a bill requiring presidential certification of human rights progress by El Salvador as a condition of continuing United States aid) had expired by its own terms shortly after the court of appeals had rendered its decision.

103. What was the line item veto?

The Line Item Veto Act of 1996 gave the President the authority to cancel certain new spending or entitlement projects, as well as the authority to cancel certain types of limited, targeted tax breaks. The President could make these cancellations within five days of the enactment of a money bill providing for such funds. These line item vetoes could then be subject to a two-thirds veto override by each the House and Senate. President Clinton used the line item veto to make 82 cancellations, and Congress overrode 38 of the cancellations, all within a single military construction bill.

In 1998, in *Clinton* v. *City of New York*, the Supreme Court held the line item veto unconstitutional, in violation of the Presentment Clause, found in Article I, section 7 of the Constitution. The Presentment Clause requires that every bill that passes the House and Senate must be presented to the President for either approval or disapproval. According to Justice John Paul Stevens, writing for the majority, this clause was violated because the line item veto authority gave the President a power which was “the functional equivalent of partial repeals of acts of Congress,” and the Constitution makes no such provision for this.

104. What is the date for the commencement of a President’s term and how is it set?

When the Constitution was ratified, Congress was given power to determine the date for beginning the operations of the new administration. Congress set the date of March 4, 1789. Although George Washington did not take the oath of office until April 30, 1789, his term began March 4. Later, the 20th or so-called “lame-duck” amendment, ratified in 1933, established January 20 as the date on which Presidents would be inaugurated. In 1937, President

Franklin D. Roosevelt became the first President to take the oath on January 20. When inauguration day falls on a Sunday, it is traditional practice for the President to take the oath privately on January 20 and to hold the public ceremony the following day.

105. What qualifications are prescribed for the President?

According to Article II, section 1 of the Constitution, that person must be a natural-born citizen, at least 35 years old, and a resident of the United States for at least 14 years. The question as to whether a child born abroad of an American parent is "a natural-born citizen," in the sense of this clause, has been frequently debated. While several constitutional scholars have argued that such a person should qualify as a natural-born citizen, there is no definitive answer.

106. Did any presidential candidate win the popular vote but lose election in the electoral college?

Yes. In 1876, 1888, and 2000. In 1876, Rutherford B. Hayes, a Republican, received 4,034,311 popular votes and 185 electoral college votes, as opposed to Samuel J. Tilden, a Democrat, who won 4,288,546 votes and only 184 electoral college votes. This election was further complicated by disputes over elections in Florida, Oregon, South Carolina, and Louisiana. Congress appointed a commission made up of five Senators, five representatives and five Supreme Court Justices to adjudicate the undecided and contested votes of a deadlocked electoral college. On the basis of the rulings of the congressional commission, the final electoral votes were 185 votes for Hayes and 184 for Tilden. The final tallies were not decided until March 2, 1877, two days before the inauguration. Neither candidate knew who would be President as each boarded a train for Washington the week before the inauguration.

In 1888, Benjamin Harrison, a Republican, was elected President with 233 electoral votes to Grover Cleveland's 168 votes, despite Cleveland's popular election victory of 5,534,488 votes over Harrison's 5,442,892.

In 2000, George W. Bush, a Republican, was elected President with 271 electoral votes after receiving 50,465,165 popular votes to Democrat Albert Gore, Jr.'s 266 electoral votes and 50,996,062 popular votes.

The post-election period before the electoral college met on December 18, 2000, was centered on disputes about the popular vote total in Florida. The U.S. Supreme Court decided in *Bush* v. *Gore* (531 U.S. 98) that the Florida Supreme Court's order directing a partial manual recount of the vote for presidential electors violated the Equal Protection Clause by allowing arbitrary and disparate treatment of members of the electorate.

107. How often has the election of the President passed to the House of Representatives?

Two times. In 1800, Thomas Jefferson and Aaron Burr were tied with 73 electoral votes each. The House voted in favor of Jefferson.

In 1824, Andrew Jackson won about 155,000 popular votes and 99 electoral votes, but he lacked sufficient numbers to gain a clear majority over John Quincy Adams, who won approximately 105,000 of the popular votes and only 84 electoral votes, and two additional candidates, William H. Crawford and Henry Clay, who had 78 electoral votes between them. The House voted in favor of John Quincy Adams.

108. What is the wording of the oath taken by the President? Who administers it?

The oath of office for the President is prescribed by Article II, section 1, clause 8 of the Constitution as follows: *I do solemnly swear (or affirm) that I will faithfully execute the office of President of the United States, and will, to the best of my ability, preserve, protect, and defend the Constitution of the United States.*

Usually, the Chief Justice of the Supreme Court administers the oath, although there is no provision made for this within the Constitution. In fact, other judges have administered the oath at times of unexpected presidential succession.

109. What provision is made by the Constitution or by law for execution of the duties of President in the event of death, resignation, disability, or removal from office?

The 25th amendment states:

(1) *in case of the removal of the President from office or of his death or resignation, the Vice President becomes President;*

(2) *when there is a vacancy in the office of Vice President, the President shall nominate a Vice President who shall take office upon confirmation by a majority vote of both Houses of Congress;*

(3) *whenever the President transmits to the President pro tempore of the Senate and Speaker of the House of Representatives his written declaration that he is unable to discharge the powers and duties of his office, and until he transmits to them a written declaration to the contrary, such powers and duties shall be discharged by the Vice President as Acting President;*

(4) *whenever the Vice President and a majority of either the principal officers of the executive departments or of such other body as Congress may by law provide, transmit to the President pro tempore of the Senate and Speaker of the House of Representatives their written declaration that the President is unable to discharge the powers and duties of his office, the Vice President shall immediately assume the powers and duties of the office as Acting President.*

Thereafter, when the President transmits to the President pro tempore of the Senate and the Speaker of the House of Representatives his written declaration that no inability exists, he shall resume the powers and duties of his office unless the Vice President and a majority of either the principal officers of the executive departments or such other body as Congress may by law provide, transmit within 4 days to the President pro tempore of the Senate and Speaker of the House of Representatives their written declaration that the President is unable to discharge the powers and duties of his office. Thereupon Congress shall decide the issue, assembling within 48 hours for that purpose, if not already in session. If the Congress, within 21 days after receipt of the latter written declaration, or, if Congress is required to assemble, determines by two-thirds vote of both Houses that the President is unable to discharge the powers and duties of his office, the Vice President shall continue to discharge the same as Acting President; otherwise, the President shall assume the powers and duties of his office.

110. Who would succeed to the Presidency if the office becomes vacant and there is no Vice President?

Under the Presidential Succession Act of 1947, it would be the Speaker of the House of Representatives, after resigning as Speaker and as a Representative. In the event the Speaker should not qualify, the President pro tempore of the Senate would discharge the powers and duties of the office of President. He would be required to resign from the Senate. Succession would then proceed in the following order, which has been modified over the years as new departments have been added: Secretary of State, Secretary of the Treasury, Secretary of Defense, Attorney General, Secretary of the Interior, Secretary of Agriculture, Secretary of Commerce, Secretary of Labor, Secretary of Health and Human Services, Secretary of Housing and Urban Development, Secretary of Transportation, Secretary of Energy, Secretary of Education, and Secretary of Veterans Affairs.

111. Has a President or Vice President ever resigned?

Two Vice Presidents have resigned. John C. Calhoun resigned on December 28, 1832, three months before the expiration of his term, to become Senator from South Carolina. Spiro T. Agnew resigned October 10, 1973, subsequent to pleading nolo contendere (no contest) to a charge of Federal income tax evasion. Following Mr. Agnew's resignation, President Richard Nixon nominated Gerald R. Ford, the Minority Leader of the House, to fill the Vice Presidential vacancy. The Senate and House, in accordance with the provisions of the 25th Amendment, under which Mr. Ford had been nominated, approved the nomination. He was sworn into office on December 6, 1973. Less than a year later, on August 9, 1974, Gerald Ford became President following Richard Nixon's resignation. Shortly thereafter, Mr. Ford nominated Nelson A. Rockefeller to be Vice President; he was confirmed and sworn into office on December 19, 1974. Thus, in about one year, two occasions arose for using the provisions of the 25th Amendment to fill a vacancy in the Vice Presidency.

112. How many Vice Presidents have succeeded to the Presidency by reason of a vacancy in that office?

Nine: John Tyler, Millard Fillmore, Andrew Johnson, Chester A. Arthur, Theodore Roosevelt, Calvin Coolidge, Harry S Truman, Lyndon B. Johnson, and Gerald R. Ford.

113. Of these successions, how many were caused by the assassination of Presidents?

Four: Abraham Lincoln, James A. Garfield, William McKinley, and John F. Kennedy were assassinated. Andrew Johnson served as President all but 1 month of Lincoln's second term; Theodore Roosevelt served 3½ years of McKinley's second term; Chester A.

Arthur served 3½ years of Garfield's term; and Lyndon B. Johnson served about 1¼ years of Kennedy's term.

114. What would happen if the President-elect were to die before taking office?

In the event that the President-elect dies or resigns after the electoral vote is cast, then the Vice President-elect would be sworn in as President, as provided for in the 20th Amendment.

115. How are Vice Presidents elected?

The 12th Amendment provides that the electors appointed by each State will name on distinct ballots the persons to be voted for as Vice President. A list of the electoral votes is then signed, certified, and transmitted "sealed" to the President of the U.S. Senate (i.e., the incumbent Vice President). These certificates are opened by the President of the Senate, in the presence of the Senate and House of Representatives, and the votes are then counted. The person having a majority of the Vice Presidential votes of the electors becomes Vice President. If no person has a majority, the Senate then chooses the Vice President from the two candidates receiving the largest number of votes. Two-thirds of the Senators must be present during the voting, with a majority necessary for election.

116. What are the qualifications for Vice President?

The qualifications for Vice President are the same as President. Article II, Section 4 of the Constitution provides that a President must be a natural-born citizen, at least 35 years old, and have been a resident of the United States for at least 14 years. The Vice President must meet these same criteria.

117. Does a President have any control over the sessions of Congress?

Under the Constitution the President may convene Congress, or either House, "on extraordinary occasions." It is usual for the President in calling an extra session to indicate the exact matter that needs the attention of Congress. However, once convened, a Congress cannot be limited in the subject matter that it will consider.

The President is also empowered by the Constitution to adjourn Congress "at such time as he may think proper" when the House and Senate disagree with respect to the time for adjournment. No President has exercised this power. Many constitutional experts believe the provision applies only in the case of extraordinary sessions.

118. Has it always been customary for Presidents to appear before joint sessions of the House and Senate to deliver their annual State of the Union message?

Presidents George Washington and John Adams appeared before the two Houses in joint session to read their messages. Thomas Jefferson discontinued the practice in 1801, transmitting his message to the Capitol to be read by clerks in both Chambers. Jefferson's procedure was followed for a full century. In 1913, believing that the President should make appeals to the Nation and to Congress, Woodrow Wilson personally appeared before the two Houses and delivered a special message on finance. Later that same year, he delivered the "Annual Message" before both chambers, and, with the exception of President Herbert Hoover, the practice has been followed by subsequent Presidents.

119. What is the "President's Cabinet"?

The President's Cabinet has been commonly regarded as an institution whose existence has relied more upon custom than law. Article II, section 2 of the Constitution, gives some guidance in this matter, stating that the President "may require the Opinion, in writing, of the principal Officer in each of the executive Departments, upon any subject relating to the Duties of their respective Offices." The historical origins of the Cabinet can be traced to the first President, George Washington. After the First Congress created the State, Treasury, and War Departments and established the Office of the Attorney General, Washington made appropriate appointments and, subsequently, found it useful to meet with the heads, also known as secretaries, of the executive departments. The Cabinet could act as the President's primary advisory group; in practice, however, Presidents have used it, along with other advisors and *ad hoc* arrangements, as they have seen fit.

120. What is the membership of the Cabinet?

Traditionally, the membership of the Cabinet has consisted of the heads of the executive departments. Currently, there are 15 departments: the Departments of Agriculture, Commerce, Defense, Education, Energy, Health and Human Services, Housing and Urban Development, the Interior, Justice, Labor, State, Transportation, the Treasury, Veterans Affairs, and Homeland Security.

From the earliest days, Presidents have accorded to others the privilege of attending and participating in Cabinet meetings. In recent years, the President's Chief of Staff, the Director of Central Intelligence, and the Director of the Office of Management and Budget, among others, have been accorded Cabinet rank.

The Executive Departments and Agencies

121. How are executive departments and agencies created?

Executive departments must be created by statute. By comparison, agencies in the executive branch may be created by a variety of means: statute, internal departmental reorganizations, or, in some instances, Presidential directive. Deriving from the constitutional capacity as Chief Executive, Commander in Chief, or by delegation of authority by Congress, the President can create various agencies or units by Executive order. All agencies, however, must ultimately be given a statutory authority if they are to receive appropriations or their decisions are to have legal force.

122. How are executive departments and agencies funded?

Most depend on annual appropriations passed by Congress. In some cases, though, the appropriation is permanent and requires no annual action by Congress. Certain agencies also operate from revenue received when loans are repaid and from nonappropriated funds such as money received from theaters, post exchanges on military bases, and various other types of user fees.

123. Who oversees the operations of executive departments and agencies?

Oversight of the executive departments is shared among the three branches of Government. It is exercised by Congress as a consequence of its constitutional authority to enact laws, appropriate funds, and make rules for the Government. Congress monitors departmental administration and operations and reviews past activities, in order to ensure compliance with legislative intent, among other reasons. Congressional oversight is conducted largely through the committees and subcommittees of the House of Representatives and Senate. These panels are assisted by their own staff and congressional support agencies.

The Federal courts also exert a degree of control over the executive departments through judgments as to the legality of actions or orders compelling compliance with the laws.

Within the executive branch, the President exercises control over departments and the agencies through appointments of officials, as well as through the Office of Management and Budget. In addition, other offices, such as chief financial officers and inspectors general, are involved in overseeing agency operations and activities.

124. Why is there a merit system for Federal employees?

The Federal merit system was established to ensure that any personnel actions, such as hiring, promotion, demotion, or firing, are taken on the basis of an individual's ability and performance. It replaced the "spoils system" whereby political patronage controlled hiring and firing practices. By contrast, the merit system is designed to ensure that the best candidates are hired for Federal positions, that they will be treated fairly, and that they will have the opportunity to rise as far as their abilities take them. Important merit system principles include the selection and advancement for Federal positions on the basis of knowledge, ability and skills, under fair and open competition; and personnel management conducted without regard to politics, race, color, religion, national origin, sex, marital status, age or handicapping condition.

125. Are all Federal employees covered by a merit system?

More than 90 percent of federal employees are covered under one of four merit systems. The Civil Service System is the largest merit system and is managed by the Office of Personnel Management. It covers approximately three-fifths of all Federal employees. The Senior Executive Service system covers only the upper stratum of civil servants. Some agencies, including the U.S. Postal Service and the Federal Bureau of Investigation, have separate merit systems, and these systems account for approximately 30 percent of all federal employees. The remainder of the federal employees covered by merit systems are under the Excepted Service.

126. What are the roles of the Office of Personnel Management, the Merit Systems Protection Board, and the Federal Labor Relations Authority?

The Civil Service Reform Act of 1978 created three separate agencies to replace the U.S. Civil Service Commission. The Office of Personnel Management (OPM) is the central personnel agency for the Federal Government. Among other responsibilities, it advises the President on civilian employment matters; executes, administers, and enforces civil service laws, rules, and regulations; and provides leadership and assistance to Federal agencies in carrying out Federal personnel policies.

The Merit Systems Protection Board (MSPB) is a quasi-judicial agency designed to protect the integrity of the Federal merit system against prohibited personnel practices. An Office of Special Counsel (OSC), which until 1989 was part of MSPB, but is now an independent entity, is an investigative and prosecutorial agency charged with protecting employees from prohibited personnel practices, especially reprisal for whistleblowing. The Federal Labor Relations Authority (FLRA) adjudicates labor-management disputes in Federal agencies. It is responsible for conducting hearings and deciding complaints of unfair labor practices.

INDEPENDENT AGENCIES AND COMMISSIONS

127. What are independent agencies and regulatory commissions?

In general, the independent agencies comprise all Federal administrative agencies not included under the executive departments or under the direct, immediate authority of the President. These many and diverse organizations range from regulatory commissions, to Government corporations, such as the U.S. Postal Service, to a wide variety of boards and foundations. Some of these, such as the Smithsonian Institution, are of long standing, while others have been created in recent years, as the Federal Government has increased its responsibilities. Independent regulatory commissions have been established by Congress—beginning in the 1880s with the now defunct Interstate Commerce Commission—to regulate some aspect of the U.S. economy. Among these are the Securities and Exchange Commission, the Federal Communications Commission, the Federal Trade Commission, and the Nuclear Regulatory Commission.

Such agencies are not independent of the U.S. Government and are subject to the laws that are approved by Congress and executed by the President.

128. To whom are independent agencies and commissions responsible? How do they report on their activities?

Independent regulatory commissions, Government corporations, and various other Government-sponsored enterprises are bodies headed by several commissioners, directors, or governors, who are appointed by the President and confirmed by the Senate. Unlike administrators of executive agencies, regulatory commissioners serve for fixed terms and cannot be removed at the pleasure of the

President. In some cases, Government-sponsored enterprises may also have directors who are private citizens. While all of the independent regulatory commissions and most of the Government-sponsored enterprises submit their budget requests to OMB for review and clearance, the degree of dependence on these budgets varies considerably. While nearly all of the Government-sponsored enterprises generate a substantial part of their financial resources from outside sources, almost all the independent regulatory commissions rely on the Government for their funding.

Activities of all of these entities are presented in public reports which are prepared annually. In addition, they are subject to periodic authorization and appropriations hearings in Congress, where their activities and operations can be reviewed.

THE JUDICIAL BRANCH

129. What is the "supreme law of the land"?

The Constitution, laws of the United States made pursuant to the Constitution, and treaties made under authority of the United States comprise the "supreme law of the land." Judges throughout the country are bound by them, regardless of anything in separate State constitutions or laws.

130. What is the main principle of the system of justice in the United States?

The guiding principle of the U.S. system of justice, "Equal Justice Under Law," is engraved in the marble pediment above the entrance of the U.S. Supreme Court Building.

THE COURTS OF THE UNITED STATES

131. By what authority are the Federal courts established?

Article III of the Constitution provides that there shall be one Supreme Court and such inferior courts as Congress may "ordain and establish." Additionally, Article 1, Section 8 provides that Congress has the power "to constitute tribunals inferior to the Supreme Court." The Judiciary Act of 1789 formally established the Supreme Court and Federal court system. Additional information about the federal court system may be found at *<www.uscourts.gov>*.

132. What is the highest court and how is it organized?

As mandated by the Constitution, the Supreme Court of the United States is the highest court. The Court has been composed of the Chief Justice of the United States and, since 1869, eight Associate Justices. Congress, which governs the Court's organization by legislation, varied the number of Justices between five and 10 in the period prior to 1869. Congress requires six Justices for a quorum to transact the business of the Court.

133. What is the jurisdiction of the Supreme Court?

The Constitution provides that in all cases affecting ambassadors to the United States, other public ministers and consuls, and those in which a State is party, the Supreme Court has original jurisdiction. The 11th amendment, moreover, precludes citizens of one State from suing another State. Additionally, the Constitution provides that Congress may regulate the appellate jurisdiction of the Court. Congress has authorized the Supreme Court, among other things, to review judgements of lower Federal courts and the highest courts of the States.

134. What is the process by which the Supreme Court reaches a decision and who sets this process or procedure?

The internal review process of the Court has largely evolved by custom while the procedures to be followed by petitioners to the Court are established in rules set forth by the Court.

After initially examining each case submitted, the Justices hold a private conference to decide which cases to schedule for oral argument, which to decide without argument, and which to deny. If at least four Justices agree, a case will be taken by the Court for a decision, with or without oral argument, and the other petitions for review will be denied. If oral argument is heard, the parties are generally allowed a total of one hour to argue the issues and respond to questions from the Justices. Later, in conference, the Justices make their decision by simple majority or plurality vote. A tie vote means that the decision of the lower court is allowed to stand. Such a vote could occur when one or three Justices do not take part in a decision.

135. How does the Supreme Court cope with the large number of decisions which it receives on appeal from State and Federal courts?

Each year the Court receives more than 7,000 petitions from State and lower Federal courts. While examining all of the cases submitted, the Court agrees to hear oral arguments on about 90 each term. Also, the Justices, without hearing oral arguments, decide a limited number of other cases—usually fewer than 75. The rest of the petitions are denied.

136. Who writes the opinions of the Supreme Court?

When the Justices have decided a case, the Chief Justice, if voting with the majority, may write the opinion himself or assign an Associate Justice to write the opinion of the Court. If the Chief Justice is in the minority, the senior Associate Justice in the majority may write the opinion himself or herself or assign another Associate Justice in the majority to write the opinion. The individual Justices may write their own concurring or dissenting opinions in any decision.

137. Why is so much importance placed on a Supreme Court decision?

Article VI of the Constitution provides that the Constitution and the laws of the United States made “in Pursuance thereof” shall be the supreme law of the land. Thus, when the Supreme Court decides a case, particularly on constitutional grounds, it becomes guidance for all the lower courts and legislators when a similar question arises. Under its power of judicial review, the Court can declare laws unconstitutional, thus making them null and void.

138. What are the Federal District Courts and how are they organized?

The 94 district courts, created by Congress, are the trial courts in the Federal judicial system. It is in these courts that most Federal cases are first tried and decided. There is at least one district court in each State for a total of 89 in the 50 States. In addition, there is one court for each of the following five jurisdictions: District of Columbia, Puerto Rico, Guam, the U.S. Virgin Islands, and the Northern Mariana Islands. The number of judges varies in each court from two to 28. Trials in these courts are generally heard by a single judge.

139. What are the Courts of Appeals and how are they organized?

Often called circuit courts, they are divided geographically into 12 circuits, each having from 6 to 28 judges. The jurisdiction of these courts covers appeals from the district courts and appeals from actions of Government agencies. Cases are generally presented to the courts sitting in panels consisting of three judges. There also is a Court of Appeals for the Federal Circuit with a nationwide jurisdiction, which reviews lower court rulings in, among other things, patent, trademark, and copyright cases.

140. What other Federal courts are there?

There are several special courts of the United States that have jurisdiction over specialized subjects. The jurisdiction of each court is indicated by its title: The U.S. Court of Federal Claims hears various kinds of claims against the United States; the Court of International Trade hears claims against the Government arising from Federal laws governing import transactions; the Tax Court adjudicates controversies involving deficiencies or overpayment of taxes; the U.S. Court of Appeals for the Armed Forces reviews court-martial convictions of all of the armed services; and the Court of Veterans Appeals reviews decisions of the Board of Veterans Appeals. There are a few other courts composed of regular U.S. district and appellate judges who render this service in addition to their regular duties.

THE JUSTICES AND JUDGES

141. What are the qualifications required to be a Justice of the Supreme Court?

There are neither constitutional nor statutory qualifications for appointees to the Supreme Court. Determining the qualifications of the individuals selected is left up to the President, who nominates, and the Members of the Senate, who confirm individuals to the Court.

142. What is the tenure of a Federal judge?

Judges of the Court of Federal Claims, Tax Court, Court of Appeals for the Armed Forces, and Court of Veterans Appeals have terms of 15 years, and judges of the territorial District Courts in Guam, the Virgin Islands, and the Northern Mariana Islands have 10-year terms. Otherwise, the judges of the courts mentioned in the preceding questions, including the Supreme Court, courts of appeals, and most Federal district courts, have "good behaviour" tenure as specified in the Constitution, which is generally considered to be life tenure.

143. Why do most Federal judges have "good behaviour" tenure?

The Framers of the Constitution believed that by allowing for a "good behaviour" tenure and prohibiting the diminution of a judge's compensation while in office, the independence of the Federal judiciary could be preserved. Thus, if a judicial decision displeased the Executive or legislature, or a majority of the population, the judges could not be punished for it. This judicial independence was considered to be a key part of the system of checks and balances established by the Constitution.

144. How and for what reasons may judges with "good behaviour" tenure be removed from office?

Such judges may be removed from office by impeachment for treason, bribery, or other high crimes and misdemeanors. One statute specifically states that Justices or judges appointed under the authority of the United States who engage in the practice of law are guilty of a high misdemeanor. Otherwise, it is up to Congress to determine if certain judicial misbehavior meets the understanding of a high crime and misdemeanor.

145. What is the oath of office for Federal judges and Justices?

A Federal statute provides that each Justice or judge of any court created by enactment of Congress shall take the following oath before performing the duties of office: *"I do solemnly swear (or affirm) that I will administer justice without respect to persons, and do equal right to the poor and to the rich, and that I will faithfully and impartially discharge and perform all the duties incumbent upon me as * * * under the Constitution and laws of the United States. So help me God."*

THE ELECTORAL PROCESS

146. How are Presidents and Vice Presidents of the United States nominated?

Candidates for President and Vice President are nominated either through individual declaration or by the action of a major or minor political party.

Presidential and Vice Presidential candidates nominated by the major parties are chosen at the national conventions of their respective parties. Delegates to these conventions are chosen on the State level by a variety of methods, including Presidential primaries, caucuses, conventions, or some combination of two or more of these elements. The process of delegate selection begins early in the Presidential election year, usually in late January or early February, and is completed well in advance of the national conventions, usually by June. National party conventions traditionally meet in July or August of Presidential election years, with the party "out of power" in the White House usually convening about one month prior to the other party.

The prenomination campaign may begin within the major parties as early as a candidate wishes to announce and begin organizing and fundraising. However, only funds raised after January 1 of the year preceding the Presidential election year qualify for Federal matching funds.

147. How are Presidents and Vice Presidents elected?

The President and Vice President of the United States are chosen every four years, in even-numbered years divisible by the number four, by a majority vote of Presidential electors who are elected by popular vote in each State.

Candidates for the Presidency, Vice Presidency, and the office of elector representing the major political parties are automatically accorded ballot access in all of the States, while minor party candidates must satisfy various State requirements, such as gaining a requisite degree of public support, through petition signatures, establishing a State-mandated organizational structure, or having polled a required number of votes in the most recent statewide election.

All States also provide for inclusion of independent candidates on the general election ballot. In almost every case, candidates must submit a requisite number of petitions signed by registered voters in order to gain ballot access. Some States also provide for write-in votes for candidates not included on the ballot.

Although the major political parties dominate Presidential election contests, there are usually a number of independent and minor party candidates. In 1996, for example, 19 minor party candidates for President were listed on the ballot in at least one state, including the Reform Party candidate, who received 8.4% of the popular vote. The same candidate had also run in 1992 on the Reform Party ticket and won 18.9% of the vote, the highest minor party vote total since the 1912 election, when former President Theodore Roosevelt won 27.4% as the Progressive Party candidate. None of the minor party candidates in either 1992 or 1996 won any electoral votes.

The general election campaign for independent or minor party candidates may begin as early as the candidates wish. Major-party Presidential campaigns traditionally begin on Labor Day and, therefore, last approximately two months.

148. What is the "electoral college"? What is its role in the election of the President and Vice President of the United States?

The President and Vice President of the United States are elected by electors, individuals who are chosen in the November general election in Presidential election years. The electors meet in their respective States on the first Monday after the second Wednesday in December to vote, separately, for President and Vice President.

Although the term does not appear in the Constitution, the electors are collectively known as the electoral college.

Each State is assigned a number of electors equal to the total of its Senators and Representatives in the U.S. Congress. The District of Columbia, under the 23rd Amendment, chooses a number equal to that assigned to the least populous State (three). The electoral college currently comprises 538 members when constituted. The Constitution requires that candidates for President and Vice President receive an absolute majority of electoral votes in order to be elected (270 of the current total of 538).

The Constitution, in Article II, Section 1, provides that, "No Senator or Representative, or person holding an office of trust or profit under the United States shall be appointed an elector." Aside from this disqualification, any person is qualified to be an elector for President and Vice President.

While the Constitution (Article II, Section 1) empowers the States to appoint electors "in such manner as the legislature thereof may direct," all 50 States and the District of Columbia currently provide that Presidential electors be elected by popular vote. Forty-eight States and the District of Columbia provide for winner-take-all, at-large elections, known as the general ticket system; it awards all electoral votes to the candidate who receives a plurality of popular votes cast in the State. Maine, beginning in 1972, and Nebraska, beginning in 1992, comprise the only current exceptions to this arrangement, using the district system to award electoral votes. Under the district system, popular votes are tallied in each congressional district and on a statewide basis. The popular vote winner in each district is awarded one electoral vote, while the statewide popular vote winner is awarded two additional votes, reflecting the two "senatorial" electors assigned to each State regardless of population.

The modern electoral college almost always reflects the preelection pledges of its members and does not, as the Founding Fathers anticipated, make independent judgments concerning who should be elected President and Vice President. Between 1820 and 1988, only 16 electors cast their votes for candidates other than those to whom they were pledged. This is known as the phenomenon of the "unfaithful" or "faithless" elector. While a number of States have enacted legislation that seeks to bind electors to the popular vote winners, the preponderance of opinion among constitutional scholars holds that electors remain free agents.

The electoral college never meets as one body, but in 51 State electoral colleges, usually in the State capital. Separate votes are cast for President and Vice President. Once the electors have voted and the results have been certified by the Governor of each State, the results are forwarded to the President of the U.S. Senate (the Vice President). The electoral vote certificates are opened and tallied at a joint session of Congress held on the sixth day of January succeeding every meeting of the electors, or, by custom, on the following day if the sixth falls on a Sunday, with the Vice President presiding. The winning candidates are then declared to have been elected.

If no candidate for President or Vice President has received a majority, the House of Representatives, voting by States, elects the President, and the Senate, voting as individuals, elects the Vice President.

149. Did the electoral college ever vote unanimously for any President?

The electors voted unanimously on only two occasions, both for George Washington, for the terms beginning in 1789 and 1793. In the Presidential election of 1820, all the electors except one voted to reelect James Monroe.

150. How are Senators and Representatives nominated and elected?

Senate and House candidates of major political parties are nominated by primary election in most States. Some States also provide for a party convention or committee recommendation in conjunction with a primary. In many States, no primary election is held for a particular office if the candidate is unopposed for nomination. Minor-party candidates in most States are nominated according to individual party rules and procedures. Independent candidates are nominated by self-declaration.

Major-party candidates are afforded automatic ballot access in all States, while minor-party and independent candidates must meet various State requirements, such as submission of petition signatures of registered voters, in order to be placed on the general election ballot.

Senators are elected by plurality vote of eligible voters in their State. A plurality means that the candidate with the largest number of votes, usually, but not necessarily a majority, is the victor. Representatives are elected by plurality vote in the congressional district in which they are candidates. The only major exceptions to this rule in Federal general elections is found in the District of Columbia, for its Delegate to the House, which requires that a candidate receive a majority of popular votes in order to be elected. A runoff election is scheduled in the event no candidate receives the requisite majority. In addition, Louisiana requires that all candidates, including those for the U.S. Senate and House of Representatives, compete in an all-party primary election. A candidate winning a majority of votes under this arrangement is declared elected, and the general election is canceled for that office.

151. What are the qualifications to vote in a national election?

In practice, all U.S. citizens 18 years of age or older who meet certain additional qualifications established by the States are eligible to vote in national elections.

The Constitution originally provided for a limited degree of public participation in the electoral process, requiring that Members of the House of Representatives be chosen by electors having "the Qualifications requisite for Electors of the most numerous Branch of the State Legislature"; that Senators be elected by the State legislature; and that electors for President be chosen, as previously noted, "in such a Manner as the Legislature thereof may direct."

Prior to the Civil War, State action extended the franchise to a point where all white males, 21 years of age or older, and some black males, in certain nonslave States, were eligible to vote. Since the Civil War, Congress and the States have, through a series of constitutional amendments and legislative enactments, progressively extended the franchise. The 15th Amendment (1870) guaranteed the right to vote regardless of "race, color, or previous condition of servitude"; the 17th Amendment (1913) provided for direct popular election to the Senate; the 19th Amendment (1920) extended the vote to women; the 23rd Amendment (1961) established the right to vote in Presidential elections for citizens of the District of Columbia; the 24th Amendment (1964) prohibited the payment of any tax as a prerequisite for voting in Federal elections; and the 26th Amendment (1971) extended the vote to citizens 18 years of age or older.

Since 1957, Congress has enacted laws designed to prevent racial discrimination in the election process, namely, the Civil Rights Acts of 1957, 1960, and 1964. In 1965, Congress also passed the Voting Rights Act which suspended for a stated period of time all tests and similar devices, which had been used to discriminate against minority groups, particularly black citizens. This same legislation authorized Federal officers to register voters and to observe elections to insure that there was no discrimination. In 1970, Congress extended for an additional period of time the test suspension features of the 1965 Act and reduced the residence requirements imposed by States as a prerequisite for voting for Presidential electors. The Voting Rights Act Amendments of 1970 provided for the abolition of continual residency requirements for voting in Presidential elections and required the States to provide for absentee registration and voting in Presidential elections.

In 1975, Congress again extended the Voting Rights Act; placed a permanent nationwide ban on the use of literacy tests and devices; expanded the act to provide coverage for minority groups not literate in English; and required affected States and jurisdictions to offer certain kinds of bilingual assistance to voters. Congress again extended the Voting Rights Act in 1982 and amended it, to enable jurisdictions to seek release from its coverage, but only if they could meet certain conditions. Section 2 of the Act was also amended to provide that the courts could judge an election law to be discriminatory without proof that it was intended to be so, so long as the law resulted in abridging or diluting minority voting power.

The Uniformed and Overseas Citizens Absentee Voting Act of 1987 guarantees the right of persons in military service or living abroad to vote by absentee ballot in Federal elections. The Voting Accessibility for the Elderly and Handicapped Act of 1984 mandates Federal standards of physical accessibility for polling places and registration sites and requires the availability of large type ballots and hearing devices for the handicapped.

Voters must also meet State requirements in order to vote, the most common of which is registration. Citizens in 46 States and the District of Columbia must register between 10 and 50 days in advance of election day, while the States of Maine, Minnesota, and

Wisconsin provide for registration on election day. In addition, North Dakota does not require registration of voters, relying instead on presentation of personal identification at the polls. Thirty States and the District of Columbia require that voters be residents for a period of between 1 and 50 days prior to election day. In addition, most States bar registration and voting by convicted felons and those judged mentally incompetent.

152. Who is responsible for the administration of elections in the United States?

The administration of elections, including regulation of political parties, ballot access, and registration procedures, establishment of polling places, provision of election-day workers, counting and certification of the vote, and all costs associated with these activities, are the responsibility of the States. In performing these functions, the States are subject to the requirements of the Constitution and Federal law, as noted above.

153. How was the choice of a national election day made?

The Constitution (Article II, Section 1) provides that "Congress may determine the Time of choosing the Electors, and the Day on which they shall give their votes; which Day shall be the same throughout the United States." In 1792, Congress enacted legislation establishing the first Wednesday in December as the day on which Presidential electors were to assemble and vote, and further required the States to appoint electors within 34 days prior to the date set for the electors to vote. In 1845, Congress enacted legislation providing a uniform date for the choice of electors in all States, establishing "Tuesday next after the first Monday in the month of November of the year in which they are to be appointed."

In 1872, Congress extended the November election day to cover elections for Members and Delegates to the U.S. House of Representatives. In 1915, following ratification of the 17th amendment, which established direct popular election of Senators, the Tuesday after the first Monday in November was also designated as election day for Senators.

The decision to create a single day for the selection of Presidential electors was intended, in part, to prevent election abuses resulting from electors being selected on separate days in neighboring States. Several other reasons are also traditionally cited as being responsible for the selection of November as the time for Federal elections. In a largely rural and agrarian nation, harvesting of crops was completed by November, so farmers were able to take the time necessary to vote. Travel was also easier before the onset of winter weather throughout the northern States. Tuesday was chosen partly because it gave a full day's travel time between Sunday, which was widely observed by religious denominations as a strict day of rest, precluding most travel, and voting day. This interval was considered necessary when travel was either on foot or by horse in many areas, and the only polling place in most rural areas was at the county seat. The choice of Tuesday after the first Monday prevented elections from falling on the first day of the month, which was often reserved for court business at the county seat.

INFORMATION RESOURCES

154. What is the Office of the Federal Register?

The Office of the Federal Register was established in 1935 by the Federal Register Act and is administered by the National Archives and Records Administration. It is responsible for the periodic publication of laws or acts of Congress, Presidential documents, regulations that Federal agencies have issued under authority delegated by Congress, and the *U.S. Government Manual* (official handbook of the Federal Government). The *Manual* provides information on Federal agencies as well as on quasi-official agencies, on international organizations in which the United States participates, and on boards, committees, and commissions. The Office of the Federal Register Web site is located at <*www.nara.gov/fedreg/*>.

Laws consist of both public laws, which have general applicability in the society, and private laws, which normally affect a particular individual or organization. Each Act of Congress is numbered and published upon enactment in "slip law" or pamphlet form, and they are cumulated for each session of Congress in the *U.S. Statutes at Large.* Regulations of Government agencies, Presidential proclamations, and Executive orders having general applicability and legal effect are published in the *Federal Register,* which appears usually five times a week. All regulations currently in force are published in codified form in the *Code of Federal Regulations,* which is updated annually. Presidential speeches, statements, messages, and other materials made public by the White House are published currently in the *Weekly Compilation of Presidential Documents* and annually in the *Public Papers of the Presidents.*

155. What kinds of documents are published in the Federal Register?

Four types of documents must be published in the *Federal Register* before they are considered legally binding: (1) Presidential proclamations and Executive orders of general interest, and any other document the President submits or orders to be published; (2) every document issued under proper authority, which prescribes a penalty or course of conduct, confers a right, privilege, authority, or immunity, or which imposes an obligation relevant or applicable to the general public, members of a class of people, or persons of a locality; (3) documents or classes of documents required by Act of Congress to be filed and published; and (4) other documents deemed by the Director of the Office of the *Federal Register* to be of sufficient interest. These materials are reproduced in the *Federal Register* under one of the following sections: (1) Presidential Documents; (2) Rules and Regulations; (3) Proposed Rules; and (4) Notices. Although the *Federal Register* is unknown to many citizens, it constitutes a major means of regulating and governing the United States.

156. What are the other responsibilities of the National Archives?

Statutorily chartered in 1934, the National Archives, headed by the Archivist of the United States, maintains the historically valuable records of the Federal Government, including materials dating to the Revolutionary War era. Its staff arranges and preserves Federal records and prepares inventories, guides, and other finding aids to facilitate their use by Government personnel, scholars, and the public. Its collections are available for use in research rooms in all of its facilities, and copies may be purchased. Most of the historically valuable records in the agency's custody are maintained in facilities in the Washington, DC, area. Records that are primarily of regional or local interest, however, are maintained in 11 regional archives; and there are, as well, 10 specialized Presidential libraries, which are managed by the National Archives.

157. What are these Presidential libraries and where are they located?

The Presidential libraries managed by the National Archives began with President Franklin D. Roosevelt, but the current program was established with the Presidential Libraries Act of 1955. Under the terms of this law, a former President or heirs may purchase land, usually near the former President's birthplace or hometown, erect a library edifice, place his papers and records in it, and deed the facility to the Federal Government. These libraries and their holdings are open to both scholars and the public. Presidential libraries have been established for Herbert Hoover (West Branch, IA), Franklin D. Roosevelt (Hyde Park, NY), Harry S Truman (Independence, MO), Dwight D. Eisenhower (Abilene, KS), John F. Kennedy (Boston, MA), Lyndon B. Johnson (Austin, TX), Gerald R. Ford (Ann Arbor, MI), Jimmy Carter (Atlanta, GA), Ronald Reagan (Simi Valley, CA), and George Bush (College Station, TX). A Richard M. Nixon Presidential Library has been built (Yorba Linda, CA), but it is a private facility and has not been deeded to the Federal Government. The Nixon Presidential records, however, remain in Washington, DC, due to a special 1974 Act of Congress placing them in the custody of the Archivist. A library also is being planned for William Clinton in Little Rock, AR. Web sites for Presidential libraries maintained by the Archivist of the United States may be found at <*http://www.archives.gov/presidential_libraries/index.html*>.

158. Are there libraries across the United States that regularly receive copies of Federal Government publications as they are produced?

Many years ago, Congress recognized the desirability of making Government publications available to the public. The depository library program was created by Congress in order to promote the American public's awareness of the activities of their Government. Under this program, which is administered by the Superintendent of Documents of the Government Printing Office, nearly 1,300 libraries throughout the country receive Federal Government publications free of charge, and, in return, pledge to provide free access to all library patrons. Depository libraries are designated by law, by the Superintendent of Documents, and by Members of Congress. The Superintendent prepares lists of documents that are available to the depositories; and they, on the basis of patron interest, select publications for their collections. A congressional Member's office, a Federal Citizen Information Center, or a local reference librarian can usually help to identify the locations of depository libraries. A Government Printing Office Web site located at <*www.gpoaccess.gov/libraries.html*> may also be consulted to locate depository libraries.

159. What is the Federal Citizen Information Center Program?

Established in 1966 and managed by the Administrator of the General Services Administration, the Federal Information Center (FIC) is a single point of contact for people who have questions about Federal agencies, programs, and services. The FCIC currently responds to about 2 million calls per year via its nationwide, toll-free number: 800–334–4636. The Center is open for public inquiries from 8:00 AM to 8:00 PM ET each workday, except Federal holidays. Among the most frequent public inquiries are those having to do with workplace safety issues, State government matters, immigration and naturalization, Federal taxes, Federal employment, Government publications, disaster assistance, and consumer matters. A FIC Web site may be found at <*http://fic.info.gov*>.

160. What special information resources may be found at the Library of Congress?

The Library of Congress in Washington, DC—which was established by an act of April 24, 1800 appropriating $5,000 "for the purchase of such books as may be necessary for the use of Congress"—is now a library both for the Congress and for the Nation. It was restarted in 1814, when Congress purchased Thomas Jefferson's personal library of 6,500 books to replace the 3,000 volumes that burned in the Capitol fire during the War of 1812. The Library serves Congress in numerous ways, especially through its collections, reference resources, and research and analysis provided by the Congressional Research Service, the Law Library, and other departments and divisions.

The Library's vast multimedia holdings include books, papers, maps, prints, photographs, motion pictures, and sound recordings. Among them are the most comprehensive collections of Chinese, Japanese, and Russian language books outside Asia and the Commonwealth of Independent States; volumes relating to science and legal materials outstanding for American and foreign law; the world's largest collection of published aeronautical literature; the most extensive collection in the Western Hemisphere of books printed before 1501 A.D.; and manuscript collections relating to manifold aspects of American history and civilization, including the personal papers of the Presidents from George Washington through Calvin Coolidge. No introduction or special credentials are required for persons over high-school age to use the general reading rooms; special collections, however, may be used only by those with a serious purpose for doing so. The Library of Congress Web site is located at <*www.loc.gov*>.

161. What special information resources are found in other Federal libraries?

The national medical collection is located at the National Library of Medicine <*www.nlm.nih.gov*> in Bethesda, MD, and the national agricultural collection is housed at the National Agricultural Library <*www.nal.usda.gov*> in Beltsville, MD.

162. How may someone get access to unpublished Federal records that are still in agency files?

Enacted in 1966, the Freedom of Information Act (FOIA) statutorily established a presumptive right of the people to know about the activities and operations of the Federal departments and agencies. The law provides any person, individual or corporation, regardless of nationality, with access to identifiable, existing agency records without having to demonstrate a need or even give a reason for such a request. The burden of proof for withholding material sought by the public is placed upon the Government. The law specifies nine categories of information, including certain law enforcement records, confidential business information, and properly classified national security documents, that may permissibly be exempted from the rule of disclosure. Disputes over the accessibility of requested records may be ultimately settled in Federal court.

163. How is a request for records made under the Freedom of Information Act?

A request for records under the Freedom of Information Act should be made by letter indicating as specifically as possible what is being sought. The requester should state that he or she is using the FOI Act. This letter should be sent to the Federal agency or agencies thought to possess the desired records. The lower left-hand corner of the envelope should be marked "FOIA Request." If a special form is needed to process your request, it will be sent by the agency. An access professional from the agency may telephone to clarify the request or discuss responsive materials. A requester may also appeal if the original request is denied.

164. Must a fee be paid to make a Freedom of Information Act request?

There is no fee to make a FOI Act request. Nonetheless, an individual, who is not making a request for records for commercial, scholarly, or news media use, may be asked to pay reasonable standard charges only for document search and duplication. The law states, however, that in the case of an average individual's request, the first 2 hours of search time or the first 100 pages of duplication shall be provided free of charge. No agency may require advance payment of any fee unless the requester has previously failed to pay fees in a timely fashion, or the agency has determined that the fee will exceed $250. The law also has a public interest standard allowing the waiving of fees in whole or in part.

165. Will the Freedom of Information Act allow access to one's own personal records on file with a Federal agency?

The FOI Act provides any person with presumptive access to topical agency records. Personal access to one's own records is more effectively pursued under the Privacy Act. It provides presumptive access for U.S. citizens and permanent resident aliens to their own personal records on file with most Federal agencies. The law specifies certain categories of information, such as on-going criminal investigation records, that may be exempted from its rule of disclosure. In the event an individual finds such personal records to be erroneous, a supplemental correction may be placed in the file. Access requests under the Privacy Act are made in the same manner as FOI Act requests. The request envelope should be marked "Privacy Act Request."

166. What kinds of documents and publications are produced by Congress?

Congress produces various kinds of publications in the course of conducting its work. The daily Chamber activities and events of the House of Representatives and the Senate are recorded and published in the Congressional Record. When the committees and subcommittees of each House of Congress hold hearings on legislation, to examine some matter, or, in the case of the Senate, to consider a nomination or treaty, a transcript of these proceedings is made and is later often published. Studies and other supplemental materials aiding the hearings process are sometimes published as so-called committee prints. House and Senate reports, sequentially numbered, usually result when a committee completes action on legislation, concludes an investigation, or, in the case of the Senate, votes on a nomination or treaty. Other auxiliary materials of importance to each congressional Chamber, such as Presidential messages or official submissions by congressional officers, may be published as House or Senate documents, another sequentially numbered series. Finally, proposals introduced by Representatives and Senators are published as bills and resolutions.

Congress produces many other publications, such as the Congressional Directory, the primary source of information on the Congress. Others include the Congressional Pictorial Directory; How Our Laws Are Made; Our Flag; The Capitol; The Constitution Rules and Manual of the United States Senate; Constitution, Jefferson's Manual and Rules of the House of Representatives; high-school and college debate books; and various historical documents.

167. Where are these congressional publications available?

All Members receive a limited allotment of most congressional publications and documents. Committees also maintain a limited supply of hearings transcripts, committee prints, reports, documents, bills, and resolutions. The House and Senate each have a document room that is open to the public where bills, reports, public laws, and certain documents may be obtained free of charge. Some congressional publications and documents are available for purchase from the Superintendent of Documents of the Government Printing Office (GPO). Original or microform copies of the items may also be found, to varying extents, in major public libraries, Federal depository libraries, and university and law libraries throughout the United States. Congressional publications are available, as well, through websites of the Government Printing Office (<www.access.gpo.gov/su_docs/index>), the Library of Congress (<http://thomas.loc.gov>), and the House (<www.house.gov/>) and the Senate (<www.senate.gov/>), the latter two sites providing avenues to committee Web sites where documents may be posted.

168. How may someone obtain access to unpublished records of Congress?

Congress routinely transfers its noncurrent, unpublished official records, consisting mostly of committee files, to the Center for Legislative Archives of the National Archives. Senate records are available there 20 years after they are created, although some are opened earlier by action of the committee that created them. House records become available 30 years after their creation, with permission from the Clerk of the House. A small group of House and Senate records involving national security or personal privacy issues remain closed for 50 years. The National Archives publishes guides that provide full descriptions of these valuable collections.

The office files of individual Senators and Representatives are considered their personal property. Most Members donate their papers to a historical research institution in their home state. Guides to the locations of these papers are available from the House and Senate historical offices.

169. What is the correct form for letters to elected Federal officials?

CORRECT FORM FOR LETTERS

PRESIDENT

The President
The White House
1600 Pennsylvania Avenue, N.W.
Washington, DC 20500

Dear Mr. President:

Very respectfully,

VICE PRESIDENT

The Vice President
Old Executive Office Bldg.
17th St. & Pennsylvania Avenue, N.W.
Washington, DC 20501

Dear Mr. Vice President:

Sincerely,

SENATOR

The Honorable ____
U.S. Senate
Washington, DC 20510

Dear Senator ____

Sincerely,

REPRESENTATIVE

The Honorable ____
House of Representatives
Washington, DC 20515

Dear Mr. (Mrs. or Ms.) ____

Sincerely,

APPENDICES

GLOSSARY OF LEGISLATIVE TERMS

Act—Legislation which has passed both Houses of Congress, approved by the President, or passed over his veto, thus becoming law. Also used technically for a bill that has been passed by one House and engrossed.

Adjournment—Action taken by either House of Congress to end a legislative day, which can last longer than 24 hours. (See also *sine die*).

Advice and Consent—A process of Senate approval of executive and judicial appointments, and for treaties negotiated by the executive branch and signed by the President. Advice and consent of treaties requires approval by a two-thirds majority of Senators present and voting, while appointments require approval by a simple majority.

Amendment—A proposal by a Member (in committee or floor session of the respective Chamber) to alter the language or provisions of a bill or act. It is voted on in the same manner as a bill.

Appropriation—A formal approval to draw funds from the Treasury for specific purposes. This may occur through an annual appropriations act, an urgent or supplemental appropriations act, a continuing resolution, or on a permanent basis.

Authorization—A law creating or sustaining a program, delegating power to implement it, and outlining its funding. Following authorization, an appropriation actually draws funds from the Treasury.

Bill—Formally introduced legislation. Most legislative proposals are in the form of bills and are designated as H.R. (House of Representatives) or S. (Senate), depending on the House in which they originate, and are numbered consecutively in the order in which they are introduced during each Congress. Public bills deal with general questions and become Public Laws, or Acts, if approved by Congress and signed by the President. Private bills deal with individual matters such as claims against the Federal Government, immigration and naturalization cases, land titles, et cetera, and become private laws if approved and signed.

Bipartisanship—Cooperation between Members of both political parties in either or both Houses, or between the President and Members of Congress representing the other party in addressing a particular issue or proposal. Bipartisan action usually results when party leaders agree that an issue is of sufficient national importance as to preclude normal considerations of partisan advantage.

Budget—The President's annual proposal to Congress, submitted in January, outlining executive branch plans for Federal expenditures and revenue for the coming year. The budget is subject to substantial revision and amendment as part of its consideration by Congress.

Budget Authority—Allows Federal agencies to incur a financial liability. The basic types of budget authority are appropriations, contract authority, and borrowing authority.

Budget Resolution—House and Senate guidelines, and later caps, on budget authority and outlays. The budget resolution is not submitted to the President for approval, as it is considered a matter of internal congressional rules. Bills that would exceed budget caps are subject to a point of order, although waivers have been granted regularly in both Houses of Congress.

Calendar—A list of bills, resolutions, or other matters to be considered before committees or on the floor of either House of Congress.

HOUSE LEGISLATION IS PLACED ON ONE OF FIVE CALENDARS:

Corrections Calendar—The Speaker may place on the Corrections Calendar any bill appearing on the Union or House Calendar. Customarily, these bills are noncontroversial and are normally called on the second and fourth Tuesday of each month.

Discharge Calendar—Calendar to which written motions to discharge bills from committees are referred when the necessary 218 (a majority of the full House membership) signatures have been obtained. Matters on thc Discharge Calendar are considered on the second and fourth Monday of each month.

House Calendar—A list of public bills, and resolutions, other than revenue measures and measures appropriating money directly or indirectly, awaiting action by the House.

Private Calendar—Private bills in the House dealing with individual matters (such as claims against the Government, immigration, and land titles) are put on this calendar. The Private Calendar is called on the first and third Tuesday of each month.

Union Calendar—Bills and joint resolutions that directly or indirectly appropriate money or raise revenue are placed on this House Calendar chronologically according to the date reported from committee.

UNLIKE THE HOUSE, THE SENATE HAS ONLY TWO CALENDARS FOR MATTERS PENDING IN THE SENATE CHAMBER:

Senate Legislative Calendar—Listing of bills, both public and private, which have been reported from committee, have been discharged from committee, or which have been placed directly without referral to committee.

Senate Executive Calendar—Listing of Presidential nominations to Federal Government positions and treaties, both of which under the Constitution require the approval of the Senate.

Caucus—A meeting of Democratic Party members in the House, which elects party leaders and makes decisions on legislative business. (See also conference.)

Cloture—A parliamentary device used in the Senate (Rule 22) by which debate on a particular measure can be limited. The Senate otherwise has a tradition of unlimited debate. The action of 16 Senators is necessary to initiate a petition for cloture, and a vote of at least 60 Senators is required to invoke it. A vote of two-thirds of Senators present and voting is required to invoke cloture on any change in the rules of the Senate.

Committee—Subsidiary organizations of both Houses of Congress established for the purpose of considering legislation, conducting investigations, or carrying out other assignments, as instructed by the parent Chamber. Committee memberships are determined by party leadership in each House, with the seniority (time in service) of a Member being generally a prominent factor in committee assignments. Congressional committees generally fall into one of four categories: (1) Standing committees—Permanent organizations within each House specializing in consideration of bills falling in particular subject areas. Most of these panels establish subcommittees or other subunits to handle some of the workload and conduct hearings. Membership on committees generally reflects party strength in each House; the majority party usually provides a majority of members, and a senior member of the majority party is usually elected chair. (2) Joint committees—committees including membership from both Houses. Joint committees are usually established with a narrow jurisdiction and normally lack authority to report legislation to the floor of either House. (3) Select or special committees—committees usually established for a limited time period to perform a particular function and without authority to report legislation to the floor of its Chamber. These panels may be organized by either House, to conduct an investigation or to make a study and recommendations about a particular problem. (4) Conference committees—Ad hoc committees composed of Members of both Houses who are appointed for the specific purpose of reconciling similar bills which have passed the House and Senate in different form.

Committee of the Whole (Committee of the Whole House on the State of the Union)—A practice widely used by the House of Representatives to expedite the consideration of legislation. Advantages include lower quorum requirements (100 Members, rather than 218)—and streamlined procedures, including limitations on debate. All decisions taken in the Committee of the Whole require approval by the full House.

Conference—Republican Members' organization in the House and Senate and Democratic Members' organization in the Senate, which elects party leaders and makes decisions on legislative business. (See also caucus.)

Confirmation—Action by the Senate approving Presidential nominees for the executive branch, the Federal Judiciary, regulatory commissions, and certain other positions.

Contempt of Congress—Willful obstruction of the legislative process. Persons cited for contempt of Congress by either House or one of their committees are subject to prosecution in Federal courts.

Continuing Resolution—A joint appropriations measure providing emergency funding for agencies whose regular appropriations bill has not been passed.

Discharge Petition—Process in the House of Representatives by which a bill may be brought to the floor 30 days after referral to a committee (or 7 days in the case of the Rules Committee) by majority vote, despite the failure of the relevant committee to report it.

Filibuster—Under the Rules of the Senate and as a matter of tradition, debate on any measure or matter is generally unlimited. A filibuster is typically characterized by individual Senators or groups of Senators speaking at extended length against a pending measure, often with the objective of frustrating action on the pending legislative proposals.

Five-Minute Rule—Under House Rules, a measure considered in the Committee of the Whole is governed by the 5-minute rule. A Member offering an amendment is recognized to speak in favor of it for 5 minutes; another Member can claim 5 minutes of time to speak against the amendment. Pro forma amendments may be offered to extend debate time in additional 5-minute blocks.

Germaneness—A House rule that amendments to a bill must relate to the subject matter under consideration.

Gerrymandering—Drawing of district lines to maximize the electoral advantage of a political party or faction. The term was first used in 1812, when Efbridge Gerry was Governor of Massachusetts, to characterize the State redistricting plan.

Hearing—A meeting or session of a committee of Congress—usually open to the public—to obtain information and opinions on proposed legislation, to conduct an investigation, or oversee a program.

Joint Meeting—A meeting of both Houses of Congress, in which each Chamber recesses to meet for an occasion or ceremony, usually in the House Chamber. The Members of each Chamber agree by unanimous consent agreements to meet, but without formally adjourning the legislative session for the day. Foreign dignitaries visiting the Capitol frequently address joint meetings of the Congress.

Joint Session—A meeting of both Houses of Congress, customarily held in the House Chamber. Joint sessions are held for necessary administrative and official purposes: e.g., the purpose of counting electoral votes, attending inaugurations, and to hear presidential State of the Union messages. In recent years, concurrent resolutions have been passed to set the time and place for joint sessions. Before attending a joint session, each Chamber first adjourns its legislative session.

Lame Duck Session—A session of Congress meeting after elections have been held, but before the newly elected Congress has convened.

Legislative Day—A formal meeting of a House of Congress which begins with the call to order and opening of business and ends with adjournment. A legislative day may cover a period of several calendar days, with the Senate recessing at the end of each calendar day, rather than adjourning.

Markup—The process in which congressional committees and subcommittees amend and rewrite proposed legislation in order to prepare it for consideration on the floor.

Memorial—A petition to Congress from State legislatures, usually requesting some sort of legislation, or expressing the sense of the State legislature on a particular question.

Nomination—Two distinct uses of this term are: (1) the process by which candidates for an elected office gain political party approval and status as the party nominee on the general election ballot; (2) appointments to office by the President that are subject to Senate confirmation.

One-Hour Rule—The rule stipulating debate limits in the House of Representatives. Measures brought up for consideration in the House are debated for 1 hour, with the majority supporters of the bill customarily yielding half of the debate time to the opposing party.

One-Minute Speech—By custom (and not by rule of the House), Members may be recognized at the beginning of a daily session, after the Chaplain's prayer, the Pledge of Allegiance, and the approval of the Journal for the previous day's session. Sometime these speeches are made at the end of the day, after legislative business. Members address the House on subjects of their choice for not more than 1 minute each.

Other Body—The practices of the House and Senate prohibit direct reference in floor debate to actions taken in the other Chamber. Members typically refer to actions taken in "the other body," rather than to name the House or Senate expressly.

Petition—A request or plea sent to one or both Houses from an organization or private citizens' group asking support of particular legislation or favorable consideration of a matter. Petitions are referred to appropriate committees for action.

Point of Order—An objection by a Member of either House that a pending matter or proceeding is in violation of the rules.

Political Action Committee (PAC)—A group organized to promote its members' views on selected issues, usually through raising money that is contributed to the campaign funds of candidates who support the group's position.

President Pro Tempore—(Latin for *the time being*). The officer who presides over the Senate when its President (the Vice President of the United States) is absent. Tradition vests this office in the senior Senator of the majority party.

Previous Question—A motion in the House to cut off debate and force a vote on a pending measure.

Public Law—A bill or joint resolution (other than for amendments to the Constitution) passed by both Houses of Congress and approved by the President. Bills and joint resolutions vetoed by the President, but overridden by the Congress also become public law.

Quorum—The number of Members in each House necessary to conduct business (218 in the House, 100 in the Committee of the Whole, 51 in the Senate).

Ratification—Two uses of this term are: (1) the act of approval of a proposed constitutional amendment by the legislatures of the States; (2) the Senate process of advice and consent to treaties negotiated by the President.

Reapportionment—The process by which seats in the House of Representatives are reassigned among the States to reflect population changes following the decennial census.

Recess—An interruption in the session of the House or Senate of a less formal nature than an adjournment. Typically, the Senate recesses at the end of most daily sessions in order to move more quickly into legislative business when it convenes again. In the House, the Speaker is authorized to declare short-term recesses during the daily session, but the House typically adjourns at the end of each day's meeting.

Redistricting—The process within the States of redrawing legislative district boundaries to reflect population changes following the decennial census.

Report—The printed record of a committee's actions, including its votes, recommendations, and views on a bill or question of public policy or its findings and conclusions based on oversight inquiry, investigation, or other study.

Resolution—A proposal approved by either or both Houses which, except for joint resolutions signed by the President, does not have the force of law. Resolutions generally fall into one of three categories: (1) Simple resolutions, designated H. Res. or S. Res., deal with matters entirely within the prerogatives of the respective House. (2) Concurrent resolutions, designated H. Con. Res., or S. Con. Res., must be passed by both Houses, but are not presented for signature by the President. Concurrent resolutions generally are used to make or amend rules applicable to both Houses, or to express the sentiment of the two Houses. (3) Joint Resolutions, designated H.J. Res. or S.J. Res., require the approval of both Houses, and, with one exception, the signature of the President, and have the force of law if approved. There is no real difference between a bill and a joint resolution. The latter is generally used in dealing with limited matters, such as a single appropriation for a specific purpose, or for the declaration of war. Joint resolutions are also used to propose amendments to the Constitution, but these do not require the President's signature.

Rider—An unrelated amendment attached to a pending bill in order to improve its chances for passage. Requirements of germaneness limit the use of riders in House bills.

Session—The period during which Congress assembles and carries on its regular business. Each Congress generally has two regular sessions, based on the constitutional mandate that Congress assemble at least once each year. In addition, the President is empowered to call Congress into special session.

Sine Die—The final adjournment (sine die being translated from Latin literally as "without a day") used to conclude a session of Congress.

Special Rule—Also known as a "rule from the Rules Committee." Special rules are presented in the form of a House resolution by the Rules Committee to make House consideration of a particular bill in order, to set time limits for debate, and to regulate which amendments, if any, may be offered during House or Committee of the Whole consideration of the measure. Special rules are agreed to by the House by majority vote.

Statute Law—Bills and joint resolutions (except for those proposing constitutional amendments) enacted by Congress and approved by the President (or his veto overridden).

Suspension of the Rules—A House procedure which expedites consideration of legislation by limiting debate on a bill and prohibiting floor amendments, but which also requires a two-thirds majority for passage.

Tabling Motion—A motion to stop action on a pending proposal and to lay it aside indefinitely. When the Senate or House agrees to a tabling motion, the measure which has been tabled is effectively defeated.

Unanimous Consent—A practice in the House and Senate to set aside a rule of procedure, so as to expedite proceedings. It is usually connected with noncontroversial matters.

Unanimous Consent Agreement—An agreement in the Senate, formulated by party leaders and other Senators, to regulate when important bills will be taken up on the floor and to limit debate on amendments. Sometimes referred to as a "time-limitation" agreement.

Veto—The constitutional procedure by which the President refuses to approve a bill or joint resolution and thus prevents its enactment into law. A regular veto occurs when the President returns the legislation to the originating House without approval. It can be overridden only by a two-thirds vote in each House. A pocket veto occurs after Congress has adjourned and is unable to override the President's action.

SELECTIVE BIBLIOGRAPHY AND REFERENCES

Alexander, De Alva Stanwood. *History and Procedure of the House of Representatives.* New York, B. Franklin, 1970 [Reprint of 1916 edition].

Baker, Ross K. *House and Senate.* New York, W.W. Norton, 1995 (2nd ed.).

Bibby, John F. *Politics, Parties, and Elections in America.* Chicago, Nelson-Hall, 1999 (4th ed.).

Biographical Directory of the United States Congress, 1774–1996: Congressional Quarterly, Washington, DC, 1997.

Byrd, Robert C. *The Senate, 1789–1989.* Washington, DC, U.S. Govt. Print. Off., 1988–1991. 2 vols.

Chandler, Ralph Clark (ed.). *A Centennial History of the American Administrative State.* New York, The Free Press, 1987.

Cigler, Allan J. and Burdett A. Loomis (eds.). *Interest Group Politics.* Washington, DC, Congressional Quarterly Press, 1998 (5th ed.).

Congress and the President: Invitation to Struggle. Annals of the American Academy of Political and Social Science, v. 499, September 1988.

Congressional Quarterly. *Guide to the Congress,* 4th edition. Washington, DC, Congressional Quarterly, 1991.

———. *Guide to the Presidency,* 2nd edition. Washington, DC, Congressional Quarterly, 1996.

———. Guide to the U.S. Supreme Court, 3rd edition. Washington, DC, Congressional Quarterly, 1997.

The Constitution of the United States of America: Analysis and Interpretation: Annotations of Cases Decided by the Supreme Court of the United States to July 2, 1992. Prepared by the Congressional Research Service, Library of Congress. Washington, DC, U.S. Govt. Print. Off., 1996 (Senate Document 103–6, 103rd Congress, 1st Sess.).

Corwin, Edward S. *The President: Office and Powers, 1787–1984.* New York, New York University Press, 1984 (5th rev. ed.).

Corwin, Edward S. and J.W. Peltason. *Understanding the Constitution.* New York, Holt, Rinehart and Winston, 1988.

Davidson, Roger H. and Walter J. Oleszek. *Congress and Its Members.* Washington, DC, Congressional Quarterly Press, 1998.

Diamond, Martin. *The Founding of the Democratic Republic.* Itasca, IL, F.E. Peacock Publishers, 1981.

Encyclopedia of the American Constitution. New York, Macmillan Publishing Company, 1986.

Encyclopedia of the American Judicial System. New York, Charles Scribner's Sons, 1987.

Encyclopedia of the American Legislative System. New York, Charles Scribner's Sons, 1994.

Encyclopedia of the American Presidency. New York, Simon and Schuster, 1994.

Encyclopedia of the United States Congress. New York, Simon and Schuster, 1995.

Farrand, Max. *The Framing of the Constitution of the United States.* New Haven, CT, Yale University Press, 1913.

The Federalist. [1787–88] by Alexander Hamilton, James Madison, and John Jay. Edited by Benjamin Fletcher Wright. Cambridge, MA, Belknap Press of Harvard University Press, 1961.

Fesler, James W. and Donald F. Kettl. *The Politics of the Administrative Process.* Chatham, NJ, Chatham House, 1996 (2nd ed.).

Fisher Louis. *The Politics of Shared Power.* College Station, TX, Texas A&M University Press, 1998 (4th ed.).

Hernon, Peter, *et al. U.S. Government on the Web: Getting the Information You Need.* Englewood, CO, Libraries Unlimited, 1999.

Hofstadter, Richard. *The American Political Tradition and the Men Who Made It.* Foreword by Christopher Lasch. New York, Vintage Books, 1974 [cl948].

Hutson, James H. *To Make All Laws: The Congress of the United States, 1789–1989.* Boston, Houghton Mifflin, 1990.

Jones, Charles O. *Separate But Equal Branches: Congress and the Presidency.* New York, Chatham House, 1999 (2nd ed.).

Key, V.0. *Public Opinion and American Democracy.* New York, Alfred A. Knopf, 1961.

Kurian, George Thomas (ed.). *A Historical Guide to the U.S. Government.* New York, Oxford University Press, 1998.

Light, Paul C. *The Tides of Reform: Making Government Work, 1945–1995.* New Haven, CT, Yale University Press, 1997.

Lowi, Theodore. *The End of Liberalism: The Second Republic of the United States.* New York, Norton, 1979 (2nd ed.).

———. *The End of the Republic Era.* Norman, OK, University of Oklahoma Press, 1995.

Neustadt, Richard E. *Presidential Power and the Modern Presidents: The Politics of Leadership from Roosevelt to Reagan.* New York, Free Press, 1990.

Oleszek, Walter J. *Congressional Procedures and the Policy Process.* Washington, DC, Congressional Quarterly Press, 1996 (4th ed.).

Seidman, Harold. *Politics, Position, and Power: The Dynamics of Federal Organization.* New York, Oxford University Press, 1998 (5th ed.).

Tocqueville, Alexis de. *Democracy in America.* Edited by J.P. Mayer. [Two volumes in one. Based on 13th edition, 1850] Garden City, NY, Anchor Books, Doubleday & Company, Inc., 1969.

Van Riper, Paul P. *History of the United States Civil Service.* Evanston, IL, Row, Peterson, and Co., 1958.

Waldo, Dwight. *The Administrative State.* New York, Holmes and Meier, 1984 (rev. ed.).

White, Leonard D. [Four studies in administrative history] *The Federalists. The Jacksonians. The Jeffersonians.* and *The Republican Era, 1869–1901.* New York, Macmillan, 1948, 1951, 1951, and 1958, respectively.

Wilson, Woodrow. *Congressional Government.* Boston, Houghton, Mifflin, 1885.

———. *Constitutional Government in the United States.* New York, Columbia University Press, 1908.

World Wide Web Sites:

www.congress.gov [Legislative Information System of Congress]

www.fedworld.gov [clearinghouse for information at many federal sites]

www.loc.gov [Library of Congress site, including Thomas and legislation]

www.nara.gov/fedreg [Office of Federal Register publications]

www.uscourts.gov [federal judiciary, including Supreme Court]

www.whitehouse.gov [White House and presidential activities].

STATE APPORTIONMENT AND HOUSE APPORTIONMENT

[Based on the 2000 Census]

State	1990 Census		2000 Census					Seat change from 1990	2003 average district pop. [d]
	Apportion-ment pop. [a]	Seats	Apportion-ment pop. [b]	Overseas federal	Change from 1990: Total	Change from 1990: Percent	Seats [c]		
Alabama	4,040,587	7	4,461,130	14,030	420,543	10.41	7	....	635,300
Alaska	550,043	1	628,933	2,001	78,890	14.34	1	....	626,932
Arizona	3,665,228	6	5,140,683	10,051	1,475,455	40.26	8	+2	641,329
Arkansas	2,350,725	4	2,679,733	6,333	329,008	14.00	4	....	668,350
California	29,760,021	52	33,930,798	59,150	4,170,777	14.01	53	1	639,088
Colorado	3,294,394	6	4,311,882	10,621	1,017,488	30.89	7	+1	614,466
Connecticut	3,287,116	6	3,409,535	3,970	122,419	3.72	5	−1	681,113
Delaware	666,168	1	785,068	1,468	118,900	17.85	1	....	783,600
Florida	12,937,926	23	16,028,890	46,512	3,090,964	23.89	25	+2	639,295
Georgia	6,478,216	11	8,206,975	20,522	1,728,759	26.69	13	+2	629,727
Hawaii	1,108,229	2	1,216,642	5,105	108,413	9.78	2	....	605,768
Idaho	1,006,749	2	1,297,274	3,321	290,525	28.86	2	....	646,976
Illinois	11,430,602	20	12,439,042	19,749	1,008,440	8.82	19	−1	653,647
Indiana	5,544,159	10	6,090,782	10,297	546,623	9.86	9	−1	675,609
Iowa	2,776,755	5	2,931,923	5,599	155,168	5.59	5	....	585,265
Kansas	2,477,574	4	2,693,824	5,406	216,250	8.73	4	....	672,104
Kentucky	3,685,296	6	4,049,431	7,662	364,135	9.88	6	....	673,628
Louisiana	4,219,973	7	4,480,271	11,295	260,298	6.17	7	....	638,425
Maine	1,227,928	2	1,277,731	2,808	49,803	4.06	2	....	637,462
Maryland	4,781,468	8	5,307,886	11,400	526,418	11.01	8	....	662,061
Massachusetts	6,016,425	10	6,355,568	6,471	339,143	5.64	10	....	634,910
Michigan	9,295,297	16	9,955,829	17,385	660,532	7.11	15	−1	662,563
Minnesota	4,375,099	8	4,925,670	6,191	550,571	12.58	8	....	614,935
Mississippi	2,573,216	5	2,852,927	8,269	279,711	10.87	4	−1	711,164
Missouri	5,117,073	9	5,606,260	11,049	489,187	9.56	9	....	621,690
Montana	799,065	1	905,316	3,121	106,251	13.30	1	....	902,195
Nebraska	1,578,385	3	1,715,369	4,106	136,984	8.68	3	....	570,421
Nevada	1,201,833	2	2,002,032	3,775	800,199	66.58	3	+1	666,086
New Hampshire	1,109,252	2	1,238,415	2,629	129,163	11.64	2	....	617,893
New Jersey	7,730,188	13	8,424,354	10,004	694,166	8.98	13	....	647,258
New Mexico	1,515,069	3	1,823,821	4,775	308,752	20.38	3	....	606,349

STATE APPORTIONMENT AND HOUSE APPORTIONMENT—Continued

[Based on the 2000 Census]

State	1990 Census		2000 Census					Seat change from 1990	2003 average district pop. [d]
	Apportionment pop. [a]	Seats	Apportionment pop. [b]	Overseas federal	Change from 1990		Seats [c]		
					Total	Percent			
New York	17,990,455	31	19,004,973	28,516	1,014,518	5.64	29	−2	654,361
North Carolina	6,628,637	12	8,067,673	18,360	1,439,036	21.71	13	+1	619,178
North Dakota	638,800	1	643,756	1,556	4,956	0.78	1	....	642,200
Ohio	10,847,115	19	11,374,540	21,400	527,425	4.86	18	−1	630,730
Oklahoma	3,145,585	6	3,458,819	8,165	313,234	9.96	5	−1	690,131
Oregon	2,842,321	5	3,428,543	7,144	586,222	20.62	5	....	684,280
Pennsylvania	11,881,643	21	12,300,670	19,616	419,027	3.53	19	−2	646,371
Rhode Island	1,003,464	2	1,049,662	1,343	46,198	4.60	2	....	524,160
South Carolina	3,486,703	6	4,025,061	13,049	538,358	15.44	6	....	668,669
South Dakota	696,004	1	756,874	2,030	60,870	8.75	1	....	754,844
Tennessee	4,877,185	9	5,700,037	10,754	822,852	16.87	9	....	632,143
Texas	16,986,510	30	20,903,994	52,174	3,917,484	23.06	32	+2	651,619
Utah	1,722,850	3	2,236,714	2,545	513,864	29.83	3	....	744,390
Vermont	562,758	1	609,890	1,063	47,132	8.38	1	....	608,827
Virginia	6,187,358	11	7,100,702	22,187	913,344	14.76	11	....	643,501
Washington	4,866,692	9	5,908,684	14,563	1,041,992	21.41	9	....	654,902
West Virginia	1,793,477	3	1,813,077	4,733	19,600	1.09	3	....	602,781
Wisconsin	4,891,769	9	5,371,210	7,535	479,441	9.80	8	−1	670,459
Wyoming	453,588	1	495,304	1,522	41,716	9.20	1	....	493,782
Total	248,102,973	435	281,424,17?	574,330	33,321,204	13.43	435	....	....

[a] "U.S. Congress, House, Apportionment Population and State Representation, H. Doc. 102–18, 102nd Cong., 1st sess., (Washington: GPO, 1991), pp. 3,4.

[b] U.S. Dept. of Commerce, Bureau of the Census, Census 2000 Shows Resident Population of 281,421,906; Apportionment Counts Delivered to President, Press Release CB00–CN.64 (Washington, Dec. 28, 2000), Table 1. (Please note that resident population total does not include the foreign-based military and other federal employees included in the apportionment population.)

[c] Article 1, Section 2 of the Constitution establishes the minimum size of the House (one Representative per state), and a maximum (one for every 30,000 persons). Based on the 2000 Census, the House could be as few as 50 Representatives, and as many as 9,380 Representatives.

[d] The average size congressional district for each state is calculated on the resident population for each state (which is the apportionment population minus the overseas military (and other federal) employees. In 2003, the nationwide mean population for a district was 645,632, the median was 642,850, the minimum population was 493,782 and the maximum was 902,195.

POLITICAL DIVISIONS OF THE SENATE AND HOUSE FROM 1855 TO 2003

[All Figures Reflect Immediate Result of Elections. Figures Supplied by the Clerk of the House]

Congress	Years	SENATE					HOUSE OF REPRESENTATIVES				
		No. of Senators	Democrats	Republicans	Other parties	Vacancies	No. of Representatives	Democrats	Republicans	Other parties	Vacancies
34th	1855–1857	62	42	15	5	....	234	83	108	43	....
35th	1857–1859	64	39	20	5	....	237	131	92	14	....
36th	1859–1861	66	38	26	2	....	237	101	113	23	....
37th	1861–1863	50	11	31	7	1	178	42	106	28	2
38th	1863–1865	51	12	39	....	....	183	80	103	....	....
39th	1865–1867	52	10	42	....	....	191	46	145	....	....
40th	1867–1869	53	11	42	....	....	193	49	143	....	1
41st	1869–1871	74	11	61	....	2	243	73	170	....	....
42d	1871–1873	74	17	57	....	....	243	104	139	....	....
43d	1873–1875	74	19	54	....	1	293	88	203	....	2
44th	1875–1877	76	29	46	....	1	293	181	107	3	2
45th	1877–1879	76	36	39	1	....	293	156	137	....	....
46th	1879–1881	76	43	33	....	....	293	150	128	14	1
47th	1881–1883	76	37	37	2	....	293	130	152	11	....
48th	1883–1885	76	36	40	....	....	325	200	119	6	....
49th	1885–1887	76	34	41	....	1	325	182	140	2	1
50th	1887–1889	76	37	39	....	....	325	170	151	4	....
51st	1889–1891	84	37	47	....	....	330	156	173	1	....
52d	1891–1893	88	39	47	2	....	333	231	88	14	....
53d	1893–1895	88	44	38	3	3	356	220	126	10	....
54th	1895–1897	88	39	44	5	....	357	104	246	7	....
55th	1897–1899	90	34	46	10	....	357	134	206	16	1
56th	1899–1901	90	26	53	11	....	357	163	185	9	....
57th	1901–1903	90	29	56	3	2	357	153	198	5	1
58th	1903–1905	90	32	58	....	....	386	178	207	....	1
59th	1905–1907	90	32	58	....	....	386	136	250	....	....
60th	1907–1909	92	29	61	....	2	386	164	222	....	....
61st	1909–1911	92	32	59	....	1	391	172	219	....	....
62d	1911–1913	92	42	49	....	1	391	228	162	1	....
63d	1913–1915	96	51	44	1	....	435	290	127	18	....
64th	1915–1917	96	56	39	1	....	435	231	193	8	3
65th	1917–1919	96	53	42	1	....	435	[1] 210	216	9	....
66th	1919–1921	96	47	48	1	....	435	191	237	7	....
67th	1921–1923	96	37	59	....	....	435	132	300	1	2
68th	1923–1925	96	43	51	2	....	435	207	225	3	....
69th	1925–1927	96	40	54	1	1	435	183	247	5	....
70th	1927–1929	96	47	48	1	....	435	195	237	3	....
71st	1929–1931	96	39	56	1	....	435	163	267	1	4
72d	1931–1933	96	47	48	1	....	435	[2] 216	218	1	
73d	1933–1935	96	59	36	1	....	435	313	117	5	....
74th	1935–1937	96	69	25	2	....	435	322	103	10	....
75th	1937–1939	96	75	17	4	....	435	333	89	13	....
76th	1939–1941	96	69	23	4	....	435	262	169	4	....
77th	1941–1943	96	66	28	2	....	435	267	162	6	....
78th	1943–1945	96	57	38	1	....	435	222	209	4	....
79th	1945–1947	96	57	38	1	....	435	243	190	2	....
80th	1947–1949	96	45	51	....	....	435	188	246	1	....
81st	1949–1951	96	54	42	....	....	435	263	171	1	....
82d	1951–1953	96	48	47	1	....	435	234	199	2	....
83d	1953–1955	96	46	48	2	....	435	213	221	1	....
84th	1955–1957	96	48	47	1	....	435	232	203	....	....
85th	1957–1959	96	49	47	....	....	435	234	201	....	....
86th	1959–1961	98	64	34	....	....	[3] 436	283	153	....	....
87th	1961–1963	100	64	36	....	....	[4] 437	262	175	....	....
88th	1963–1965	100	67	33	....	....	435	258	176	....	1
89th	1965–1967	100	68	32	....	....	435	295	140	....	....
90th	1967–1969	100	64	36	....	....	435	248	187	....	....
91st	1969–1971	100	58	42	....	....	435	243	192	....	....
92d	1971–1973	100	54	44	2	....	435	255	180	....	....

POLITICAL DIVISIONS OF THE SENATE AND HOUSE FROM 1855 TO 2003—Continued

[All Figures Reflect Immediate Result of Elections. Figures Supplied by the Clerk of the House]

Congress	Years	SENATE					HOUSE OF REPRESENTATIVES				
		No. of Senators	Democrats	Republicans	Other parties	Vacancies	No. of Representatives	Democrats	Republicans	Other parties	Vacancies
93d	1973–1975	100	56	42	2	....	435	242	192	1	....
94th	1975–1977	100	60	37	2	....	435	291	144	1	....
95th	1977–1979	100	61	38	1	....	435	292	143	....	....
96th	1979–1981	100	58	41	1	....	435	277	158	....	....
97th	1981–1983	100	46	53	1	....	435	242	192	1	....
98th	1983–1985	100	46	54	....	....	435	269	166	....	....
99th	1985–1987	100	47	53	....	....	435	253	182	....	....
100th	1987–1989	100	55	45	....	....	435	258	177	....	....
101st	1989–1991	100	55	45	....	....	435	260	175	....	....
102d	1991–1993	100	56	44	....	....	435	267	167	1	....
103d	1993–1995	100	57	43	....	....	435	258	176	1	....
104th	1995–1997	100	48	52	....	....	435	204	230	1	....
105th	1997–1999	100	45	55	....	....	435	207	226	2	....
106th	1999–2001	100	45	55	....	....	435	211	223	1	....
107th	2001–2003	100	50	50	....	....	435	212	221	2	....
108th	2003–2005	100	48	51	1	....	435	204	229	1	1

[1] Democrats organized House with help of other parties.
[2] Democrats organized House because of Republican deaths.
[3] Proclamation declaring Alaska a State issued January 3, 1959.
[4] Proclamation declaring Hawaii a State issued August 21, 1959.

IN CONGRESS, JULY 4, 1776.

THE UNANIMOUS

DECLARATION

OF THE

THIRTEEN UNITED STATES OF AMERICA.

WHEN in the Course of human Events, it becomes necessary for one People to dissolve the Political Bands which have connected them with another, and to assume among the Powers of the Earth, the separate and equal Station to which the Laws of Nature and of Nature's God entitle them, a decent Respect to the Opinions of Mankind requires that they should declare the causes which impel them to the Separation.

WE hold these Truths to be self-evident, that all Men are created equal, that they are endowed by their Creator with certain unalienable Rights, that among these are Life, Liberty, and the Pursuit of Happiness—That to secure these Rights, Governments are instituted among Men, deriving their just Powers from the Consent of the Governed, that whenever any Form of Government becomes destructive of these Ends, it is the Right of the People to alter or to abolish it, and to institute new Government, laying its Foundation on such Principles, and organizing its Powers in such Form, as to them shall seem most likely to effect their Safety and Happiness. Prudence, indeed, will dictate that Governments long established should not be changed for light and transient Causes; and accordingly all Experience hath shewn, that Mankind are more disposed to suffer, while Evils are sufferable, than to right themselves by abolishing the Forms to which they are accustomed. But when a long Train of Abuses and Usurpations, pursuing invariably the same Object, evinces a Design to reduce them under absolute Despotism, it is their Right, it is their Duty, to throw off such Government, and to provide new Guards for their future Security. Such has been the patient Sufferance of these Colonies; and such is now the Necessity which constrains them to alter their former Systems of Government. The History of the present King of Great-Britain is a History of repeated Injuries and Usurpations, all having in direct Object the Establishment of an absolute Tyranny over these States. To prove this, let Facts be submitted to a candid World.

HE has refused his Assent to Laws, the most wholesome and necessary for the public Good.

HE has forbidden his Governors to pass Laws of immediate and pressing Importance, unless suspended in their Operation till his Assent should be obtained; and when so suspended, he has utterly neglected to attend to them.

HE has refused to pass other Laws for the Accommodation of large Districts of People, unless those People would relinquish the Right of Representation in the Legislature, a Right inestimable to them, and formidable to Tyrants only.

HE has called together Legislative Bodies at Places unusual, uncomfortable, and distant from the Depository of their public Records, for the sole Purpose of fatiguing them into Compliance with his Measures.

HE has dissolved Representative Houses repeatedly, for opposing with manly Firmness his Invasions on the Rights of the People.

HE has refused for a long Time, after such Dissolutions, to cause others to be elected; whereby the Legislative Powers, incapable of Annihilation, have returned to the People at large for their exercise; the State remaining in the mean time exposed to all the Dangers of Invasion from without, and Convulsions within.

HE has endeavoured to prevent the Population of these States; for that Purpose obstructing the Laws for Naturalization of Foreigners; refusing to pass others to encourage their Migrations hither, and raising the Conditions of new Appropriations of Lands.

HE has obstructed the Administration of Justice, by refusing his Assent to Laws for establishing Judiciary Powers.

HE has made Judges dependent on his Will alone, for the Tenure of their Offices, and the Amount and Payment of their Salaries.

HE has erected a Multitude of new Offices, and sent hither Swarms of Officers to harrass our People, and eat out their Substance.

HE kept among us, in Times of Peace, Standing Armies, without the consent of our Legislatures.

HE has affected to render the Military independent of and superior to the Civil Power.

HE has combined with others to subject us to a Jurisdiction foreign to our Constitution, and unacknowledged by our Laws; giving his Assent to their Acts of pretended Legislation:

FOR quartering large Bodies of Armed Troops among us:

FOR protecting them, by a mock Trial, from Punishment for any Murders which they should commit on the Inhabitants of these States:

FOR cutting off our Trade with all Parts of the World:

FOR imposing Taxes on us without our Consent:

FOR depriving us, in many Cases, of the Benefits of Trial by Jury:

FOR transporting us beyond Seas to be tried for pretended Offences:

FOR abolishing the free System of English Laws in a neighbouring Province, establishing therein an arbitrary Government, and enlarging its Boundaries, so as to render it at once an Example and fit Instrument for introducing the same absolute Rule into these Colonies:

FOR taking away our Charters, abolishing our most valuable Laws, and altering fundamentally the Forms of our Governments:

FOR suspending our own Legislatures, and declaring themselves invested with Power to legislate for us in all Cases whatsoever.

HE has abdicated Government here, by declaring us out of his Protection and waging War against us.

HE has plundered our Seas, ravaged our Coasts, burnt our Towns, and destroyed the Lives of our People.

HE is, at this Time, transporting large Armies of foreign Mercenaries to compleat the Works of Death, Desolation, and Tyranny, already begun with circumstances of Cruelty and Perfidy, scarcely paralleled in the most barbarous Ages, and totally unworthy the Head of a civilized Nation.

HE has constrained our fellow Citizens taken Captive on the high Seas to bear Arms against their Country, to become the Executioners of their Friends and Brethren, or to fall themselves by their Hands.

HE has excited domestic Insurrections amongst us, and has endeavoured to bring on the Inhabitants of our Frontiers, the merciless Indian Savages, whose known Rule of Warfare, is an undistinguished Destruction, of all Ages, Sexes and Conditions.

IN every stage of these Oppressions we have Petitioned for Redress in the most humble Terms: Our repeated Petitions have been answered only by repeated Injury. A Prince, whose Character is thus marked by every act which may define a Tyrant, is unfit to be the Ruler of a free People.

NOR have we been wanting in Attentions to our British Brethren. We have warned them from Time to Time of Attempts by their Legislature to extend an unwarrantable Jurisdiction over us. We have reminded them of the Circumstances of our Emigration and Settlement here. We have appealed to their native Justice and Magnanimity, and we have conjured them by the Ties of our common Kindred to disavow these Usurpations, which, would inevitably interrupt our Connections and Correspondence. They too have been deaf to the Voice of Justice and of Consanguinity. We must, therefore, acquiesce in the Necessity, which denounces our Separation, and hold them, as we hold the rest of Mankind, Enemies in War, in Peace, Friends.

WE, therefore, the Representatives of the UNITED STATES OF AMERICA, in GENERAL CONGRESS, Assembled, appealing to the Supreme Judge of the World for the Rectitude of our Intentions, do, in the Name, and by Authority of the good People of these Colonies, solemnly Publish and Declare, That these United Colonies are, and of Right ought to be, FREE AND INDEPENDENT STATES; that they are absolved from all Allegiance to the British Crown, and that all political Connection between them and the State of Great-Britain, is and ought to be totally dissolved; and that as FREE AND INDEPENDENT STATES, they have full Power to levy War, conclude Peace, contract Alliances, establish Commerce, and to do all other Acts and Things which INDEPENDENT STATES may of right do. And for the support of this Declaration, with a firm Reliance on the Protection of divine Providence, we mutually pledge to each other our Lives, our Fortunes, and our sacred Honor.

JOHN HANCOCK, PRESIDENT.

SIGNERS OF THE DECLARATION OF INDEPENDENCE

According to the Authenticated List Printed by Order of Congress of January 18, 1777

John Hancock.

Georgia,	*Button Gwinnett,* *Lyman Hall,* *Geo. Walton.*	*New-York,*	*Wm. Floyd,* *Phil. Livingston,* *Frans. Lewis,* *Lewis Morris.*
North-Carolina,	*Wm. Hooper,* *Joseph Hewes,* *John Penn.*	*New-Jersey,*	*Richd. Stockton,* *Jno. Witherspoon,* *Fras. Hopkinson,* *John Hart,* *Abra. Clark.*
South-Carolina,	*Edward Rutledge,* *Thos. Heyward, Junr.,* *Thomas Lynch, Junr.,* *Arthur Middleton.*	*New-Hampshire,*	*Josiah Bartlett,* *Wm. Whipple,* *Matthew Thornton.*
Maryland,	*Samuel Chase,* *Wm. Paca,* *Thos. Stone,* *Charles Carroll, of Carrollton.*	*Massachusetts-Bay,*	*Saml. Adams,* *John Adams,* *Robt. Treat Pane,* *Elbridge Gerry.*
Virginia,	*George Wythe,* *Richard Henry Lee,* *Ths. Jefferson,* *Benja. Harrison,* *Thos. Nelson, jr.,* *Francis Lightfoot Lee,* *Carter Braxton.*	*Rhode-Island and Providence &C.,*	*Step. Hopkins,* *William Ellery.*
Pennsylvania,	*Robt. Morris,* *Benjamin Rush,* *Benja. Franklin,* *John Morton,* *Geo. Clymer,* *Jas. Smith,* *Geo. Taylor,* *James Wilson,* *Geo. Ross.*	*Connecticut,*	*Roger Sherman,* *Saml. Huntington,* *Wm. Williams,* *Oliver Wolcott.*
Delaware,	*Caesar Rodney,* *Geo. Read.*		

In CONGRESS, January 18, 1777.

ORDERED,

That an authenticated Copy of the DECLARATION of INDEPENDENCY, with Names of the MEMBERS of CONGRESS, subscribing the same, be sent to each of the UNITED STATES, and that they be desired to have the same put on RECORD.

By Order of CONGRESS,

John Hancock, *President.*

Attest. Chas Thomson, Secy

[Explanatory Note: On January 18, 1777, Congress, then sitting in Baltimore, Maryland, ordered that authenticated copies of the Declaration be sent to the States. This version was printed by Mary Katherine Goddard of Baltimore and is known as the Goddard Broadside. Earlier, on July 19, 1776, Congress had "Resolved, That the Declaration passed on the 4th, be fairly engrossed on parchment, with the title and stile of 'The unanimous declaration of the thirteen United States of America,' and the same, when engrossed, be signed by every member of Congress." The name of Thomas McKean, then a member from Delaware, however, does not appear on the Goddard Broadside, as he did not sign the engrossed copy until after January 18, 1777.]

Constitution of the United States

We the People of the United States, in Order to form a more perfect Union, establish Justice, insure domestic Tranquility, provide for the common defence, promote the general Welfare, and secure the Blessings of Liberty to ourselves and our Posterity, do ordain and establish this Constitution for the United States of America.

ARTICLE. I.

SECTION. 1. All legislative Powers herein granted shall be vested in a Congress of the United States, which shall consist of a Senate and House of Representatives.[1]

---

[1] This text of the Constitution follows the engrossed copy signed by Gen. Washington and the deputies from 12 States. The small superior figures preceding the paragraphs designate clauses, and were not in the original and have reference to footnotes.

The Constitution was adopted by a convention of the States on September 17, 1787, and was subsequently ratified by the several States, on the following dates: Delaware, December 7, 1787; Pennsylvania, December 12, 1787; New Jersey, December 18, 1787; Georgia, January 2, 1788; Connecticut, January 9, 1788; Massachusetts, February 6, 1788; Maryland, April 28, 1788; South Carolina, May 23, 1788; New Hampshire, June 21,1788.

Ratification was completed on June 21, 1788.

The Constitution was subsequently ratified by Virginia, June 25, 1788; New York, July 26, 1788; North Carolina, November 21, 1789; Rhode Island, May 29, 1790; and Vermont, January 10, 1791.

In May 1785, a committee of Congress made a report recommending an alteration in the Articles of Confederation, but no action was taken on it, and it was left to the State legislatures to proceed in the matter. In January 1786, the Legislature of Virginia passed a resolution providing for the appointment of five commissioners, who, or any three of them, should meet such commissioners as might be appointed in the other States of the Union, at a time and place to be agreed upon, to take into consideration the trade of the United States; to consider how far a uniform system in their commercial regulations may be necessary to their common interest and their permanent harmony; and to report to the several States such an act, relative to this object, as, when ratified by them, will enable the United States in Congress effectually to provide for the same. The Virginia commissioners, after some correspondence, fixed the first Monday in September as the time, and the city of Annapolis as the place for the meeting, but only four other States were representative, viz: Delaware, New York, New Jersey, and Pennsylvania; the Commissioners appointed by Massachusetts, New Hampshire, North Carolina, and Rhode Island failed to attend. Under circumstances of so partial a representation, the commissioners present a agreed upon a report, (drawn by Mr. Hamilton, of New York), expressing their unanimous conviction that it might essentially tend to advance the interests of the Union if the States by which they were respectively delegated would concur, and use their endeavors to procure the concurrence of the other States, in the appointment of commissioners to meet at Philadelphia on the Second Monday of May following, to take into consideration the situation of the United States; to devise such further provisions as should appear to them necessary to render the Constitution of the Federal Government adequate the exigencies of the Union; and to report such an act for that purpose to the United State in Congress assembled as, when agreed to by them and afterwards confirmed by the Legislatures of every State, would effectually provide for the same.

Congress, on the 21st of February, 1787, adopted a resolution in favor of a convention, and the Legislatures of those States which had not already done so (with the exception of Rhode Island) promptly appointed delegates. On the 25th of May, seven States having convened, George Washington, of Virginia, was unanimously elected President, and the consideration of the proposed constitution was commenced. On the 17th of September, 1787, the Constitution as engrossed and agreed upon was signed by all the members present, except Mr. Gerry of Massachusetts, and Messrs. Mason and Randolph, of Virginia. The president of the convention transmitted it to Congress, with a resolution stating how the proposed Federal Government should

Continued

SECTION. 2. The House of Representatives shall be composed of Members chosen every second Year by the People of the several States, and the Electors in each State shall have the Qualifications requisite for Electors of the most numerous Branch of the State Legislature.

No Person shall be a Representative who shall not have attained to the Age of twenty five Years, and been seven Years a Citizen of the United States, and who shall not, when elected, be an Inhabitant of that State in which he shall be chosen.

Representatives and direct Taxes shall be apportioned among the several States which may be included within this Union, according to their respective Numbers, which shall be determined by adding to the whole Number of free Persons, including those bound to Service for a Term of Years, and excluding Indians not taxed, three fifths of all other Persons.[2] The actual Enumeration shall be made within three Years after the first Meeting of the Congress of the United States, and within every subsequent Term of ten Years, in such Manner as they shall by Law direct. The Number of Representatives shall not exceed one for every thirty Thousand, but each State shall have at Least one Representative; and until such enumeration shall be made, the State of New Hampshire shall be entitled to chuse three, Massachusetts eight, Rhode-Island and Providence Plantations one, Connecticut five, New-York six, New Jersey four, Pennsylvania eight, Delaware one, Maryland six, Virginia ten, North Carolina five, South Carolina five, and Georgia three.

When vacancies happen in the Representation from any State, the Executive Authority thereof shall issue Writs of Election to fill such Vacancies.

The House of Representatives shall chuse their Speaker and other Officers; and shall have the sole Power of Impeachment.

SECTION. 3. The Senate of the United States shall be composed of two Senators from each State, chosen by the Legislature thereof,[3] for six Years; and each Senator shall have one Vote.

Immediately after they shall be assembled in Consequence of the first Election, they shall be divided as equally as may be into three Classes. The Seats of the Senators of the first Class shall be vacated at the Expiration of the second Year, of the second Class at the Expiration of the fourth Year, and of the third Class at the Expiration of the sixth Year, so that one third may be chosen every

---

be put in operation, and an explanatory letter. Congress, on 28th of September, 1787, directed the Constitution so framed, with the resolutions and letter concerning the same, to "be transmitted to the several Legislatures in order to be submitted to a convention of delegates chosen in each State by the people thereof, in conformity to the resolves of the convention."

On the 4th of March, 1789, the day which had been fixed for commencing the operations of Government under the new Constitution, it had been ratified by the conventions chosen in each State to consider it, as follows: Delaware, December 7, 1787; Pennsylvania, December 12, 1787; New Jersey, December 18, 1787; Georgia, January 2, 1788; Connecticut, January 9, 1788; Massachusetts, February 6, 1788; Maryland, April 28, 1788; South Carolina, May 23, 1788; New Hampshire, June 21, 1788; Virginia, June 25, 1788; and New York, July 26, 1788.

The President informed Congress, on the 28th of January, 1790, that North Carolina had ratified the Constitution November 21, 1789; and he informed Congress on the 1st of June, 1790, that Rhode Island had ratified the Constitution May 29, 1790. Vermont, in convention, ratified the Constitution January 10, 1791, and was, by an act of Congress approved February 18, 1791, "received and admitted into this Union as a new and entire member of the United States."

[2] The part of this clause relating to the mode of apportionment of representatives among the several States has been affected by section 2 of amendment XIV, and as to taxes on incomes without apportionment by amendment XVI.

[3] This clause has been affected by clause 1 of amendment XVII.

second Year; and if Vacancies happen by Resignation, or otherwise, during the Recess of the Legislature of any State, the Executive thereof may make temporary Appointments until the next Meeting of the Legislature, which shall then fill such Vacancies.[4]

No Person shall be a Senator who shall not have attained to the Age of thirty Years, and been nine Years a Citizen of the United States, and who shall not, when elected, be an Inhabitant of that State for which he shall be chosen.

The Vice President of the United States shall be President of the Senate, but shall have no Vote, unless they be equally divided.

The Senate shall chuse their other Officers, and also a President pro tempore, in the Absence of the Vice President, or when he shall exercise the Office of President of the United States.

The Senate shall have the sole Power to try all Impeachments. When sitting for that Purpose, they shall be on Oath or Affirmation. When the President of the United States is tried, the Chief Justice shall preside: And no Person shall be convicted without the Concurrence of two thirds of the Members present.

Judgment in Cases of Impeachment shall not extend further than to removal from Office, and disqualification to hold and enjoy any Office of honor, Trust or Profit under the United States: but the Party convicted shall nevertheless be liable and subject to Indictment, Trial, Judgment and Punishment, according to Law.

SECTION. 4. The Times, Places and Manner of holding Elections for Senators and Representatives, shall be prescribed in each State by the Legislature thereof; but the Congress may at any time by Law make or alter such Regulations, except as to the Places of chusing Senators.

The Congress shall assemble at least once in every Year, and such Meeting shall be on the first Monday in December,[5] unless they shall by Law appoint a different Day.

SECTION. 5. Each House shall be the Judge of the Elections, Returns and Qualifications of its own Members, and a Majority of each shall constitute a Quorum to do Business; but a smaller Number may adjourn from day to day, and may be authorized to compel the Attendance of absent Members, in such Manner, and under such Penalties as each House may provide.

Each House may determine the Rules of its Proceedings, punish its Members for disorderly Behaviour, and, with the Concurrence of two thirds, expel a Member.

Each House shall keep a Journal of its Proceedings, and from time to time publish the same, excepting such Parts as may in their Judgment require Secrecy; and the Yeas and Nays of the Members of either House on any question shall, at the Desire of one fifth of those Present, be entered on the Journal.

Neither House, during the Session of Congress, shall, without the Consent of the other, adjourn for more than three days, nor to any other Place than that in which the two Houses shall be sitting.

SECTION. 6. The Senators and Representatives shall receive a Compensation for their Services, to be ascertained by Law, and

---

[4] This clause has been affected by clause 2 of amendment XVIII.

[5] This clause has been affected by amendment XX.

paid out of the Treasury of the United States.[6] They shall in all Cases, except Treason, Felony and Breach of the Peace, be privileged from Arrest during their Attendance at the Session of their respective Houses, and in going to and returning from the same; and for any Speech or Debate in either House, they shall not be questioned in any other Place.

No Senator or Representative shall, during the Time for which he was elected, be appointed to any civil Office under the Authority of the United States, which shall have been created, or the Emoluments whereof shall have been encreased during such time; and no Person holding any Office under the United States, shall be a Member of either House during his Continuance in Office.

SECTION. 7. All Bills for raising Revenue shall originate in the House of Representatives; but the Senate may propose or concur with Amendments as on other Bills.

Every Bill which shall have passed the House of Representatives and the Senate, shall, before it become a Law, be presented to the President of the United States; If he approve he shall sign it, but if not he shall return it, with his Objections to that House in which it shall have originated, who shall enter the Objections at large on their Journal, and proceed to reconsider it. If after such Reconsideration two thirds of that House shall agree to pass the Bill, it shall be sent, together with the Objections, to the other House, by which it shall likewise be reconsidered, and if approved by two thirds of that House, it shall become a Law. But in all such Cases the Votes of both Houses shall be determined by Yeas and Nays, and the Names of the Persons voting for and against the Bill shall be entered on the Journal of each House respectively. If any Bill shall not be returned by the President within ten Days (Sundays excepted) after it shall have been presented to him, the Same shall be a Law, in like Manner as if he had signed it, unless the Congress by their Adjournment prevent its Return, in which Case it shall not be a Law.

Every Order, Resolution, or Vote to which the Concurrence of the Senate and House of Representatives may be necessary (except on a question of Adjournment) shall be presented to the President of the United States; and before the Same shall take Effect, shall be approved by him, or being disapproved by him, shall be repassed by two thirds of the Senate and House of Representatives, according to the Rules and Limitations prescribed in the Case of a Bill.

SECTION. 8. The Congress shall have Power To lay and collect Taxes, Duties, Imposts and Excises, to pay the Debts and provide for the common Defence and general Welfare of the United States; but all Duties, Imposts and Excises shall be uniform throughout the United States;

To borrow Money on the credit of the United States;

To regulate Commerce with foreign Nations, and among the several States, and with the Indian Tribes;

To establish an uniform Rule of Naturalization, and uniform Laws on the subject of Bankruptcies throughout the United States;

To coin Money, regulate the Value thereof, and of foreign Coin, and fix the Standard of Weights and Measures;

---

[6] This clause has been affected by amendment XXVII.

To provide for the Punishment of counterfeiting the Securities and current Coin of the United States;

To establish Post Offices and post Roads;

To promote the Progress of Science and useful Arts, by securing for limited Times to Authors and Inventors the exclusive Right to their respective Writings and Discoveries;

To constitute Tribunals inferior to the supreme Court;

To define and punish Piracies and Felonies committed on the high Seas, and Offences against the Law of Nations;

To declare War, grant Letters of Marque and Reprisal, and make Rules concerning Captures on Land and Water;

To raise and support Armies, but no Appropriation of Money to that Use shall be for a longer Term than two Years;

To provide and maintain a Navy;

To make Rules for the Government and Regulation of the land and naval Forces;

To provide for calling forth the Militia to execute the Laws of the Union, suppress Insurrections and repel Invasions;

To provide for organizing, arming, and disciplining, the Militia, and for governing such Part of them as may be employed in the Service of the United States, reserving to the States respectively, the Appointment of the Officers, and the Authority of training the Militia according to the discipline prescribed by Congress;

To exercise exclusive Legislation in all Cases whatsoever, over such District (not exceeding ten Miles square) as may, by Cession of particular States, and the Acceptance of Congress, become the Seat of the Government of the United States, and to exercise like Authority over all Places purchased by the Consent of the Legislature of the State in which the Same shall be, for the Erection of Forts, Magazines, Arsenals, dock-Yards, and other needful Buildings;— And

To make all Laws which shall be necessary and proper for carrying into Execution the foregoing Powers, and all other Powers vested by this Constitution in the Government of the United States, or in any Department or Officer thereof.

SECTION. 9. The Migration or Importation of such Persons as any of the States now existing shall think proper to admit, shall not be prohibited by the Congress prior to the Year one thousand eight hundred and eight, but a Tax or duty may be imposed on such Importation, not exceeding ten dollars for each Person.

The Privilege of the Writ of Habeas Corpus shall not be suspended, unless when in Cases of Rebellion or Invasion the public Safety may require it.

No Bill of Attainder or ex post facto Law shall be passed.

No Capitation, or other direct, Tax shall be laid, unless in Proportion to the Census or Enumeration herein before directed to be taken.[7]

No Tax or Duty shall be laid on Articles exported from any State.

No Preference shall be given by any Regulation of Commerce or Revenue to the Ports of one State over those of another: nor shall Vessels bound to, or from, one State, be obliged to enter, clear, or pay Duties in another.

---

[7] This clause has been affected by amendment XVI.

No Money shall be drawn from the Treasury, but in Consequence of Appropriations made by Law; and a regular Statement and Account of the Receipts and Expenditures of all public Money shall be published from time to time.

No Title of Nobility shall be granted by the United States: And no Person holding any Office of Profit or Trust under them, shall, without the Consent of the Congress, accept of any present, Emolument, Office, or Title, of any kind whatever, from any King, Prince, or foreign State.

SECTION. 10. No State shall enter into any Treaty, Alliance, or Confederation; grant Letters of Marque and Reprisal; coin Money; emit Bills of Credit; make any Thing but gold and silver Coin a Tender in Payment of Debts; pass any Bill of Attainder, ex post facto Law, or Law impairing the Obligation of Contracts, or grant any Title of Nobility.

No State shall, without the Consent of the Congress, lay any Imposts or Duties on Import or Exports, except what may be absolutely necessary for executing it's inspection Laws: and the net Produce of all Duties and Imposts, laid by any State on Imports or Exports, shall be for the Use of the Treasury of the United States; and all such Laws shall be subject to the Revision and Controul of the Congress.

No State shall, without the Consent of Congress, lay any Duty of Tonnage, keep Troops, or Ships of War in time of Peace, enter into any Agreement or Compact with another State, or with a foreign Power, or engage in War, unless actually invaded, or in such imminent Danger as will not admit of delay.

ARTICLE. II.

SECTION. 1. The executive Power shall be vested in a President of the United States of America. He shall hold his Office during the Term of four Years, and, together with the Vice President, chosen for the same Term, be elected, as follows:

Each State shall appoint, in such Manner as the Legislature thereof may direct, a Number of Electors, equal to the whole Number of Senators and Representatives to which the State may be entitled in the Congress: but no Senator or Representative, or Person holding an Office of Trust or Profit under the United States, shall be appointed an Elector.

The Electors shall meet in their respective States, and vote by Ballot for two Persons, of whom one at least shall not be an Inhabitant of the same State with themselves. And they shall make a List of all the Persons voted for, and of the Number of Votes for each; which List they shall sign and certify, and transmit sealed to the Seat of the Government of the United States, directed to the President of the Senate. The President of the Senate shall, in the Presence of the Senate and House of Representatives, open all the Certificates, and the Votes shall then be counted. The Person having the greatest Number of Votes shall be the President, if such Number be a Majority of the whole Number of Electors appointed; and if there be more than one who have such Majority, and have an equal Number of Votes, then the House of Representatives shall immediately chuse by Ballot one of them for President; and if no Person have a Majority, then from the five highest on the List the said House shall in like Manner chuse the President. But in chusing the President, the Votes shall be taken by States, the Representation from each State having one Vote; A quorum for this Purpose shall consist of a Member or Members from two thirds of the States, and a Majority of all the States shall be necessary to a Choice. In every Case, after the Choice of the President, the Person having the greatest Number of Votes of the Electors shall be the Vice President. But if there should remain two or more who have equal Votes, the Senate shall chuse from them by Ballot the Vice President.[8]

The Congress may determine the Time of chusing the Electors, and the Day on which they shall give their Votes; which Day shall be the same throughout the United States.

No Person except a natural born Citizen, or a Citizen of the United States, at the time of the Adoption of this Constitution, shall be eligible to the Office of President; neither shall any Person be eligible to that Office who shall not have attained to the Age of thirty five Years, and been fourteen Years a Resident within the United States.

In Case of the Removal of the President from Office, or of his Death, Resignation, or Inability to discharge the Powers and Duties of the said Office,[9] the Same shall devolve on the Vice President, and the Congress may by Law provide for the Case of Removal, Death, Resignation or Inability, both of the President and Vice President, declaring what Officer shall then act as President, and such Officer shall act accordingly, until the Disability be removed, or a President shall be elected.

The President shall, at stated Times, receive for his Services, a Compensation, which shall neither be encreased nor diminished during the Period for which he shall have been elected, and he shall not receive within that Period any other Emolument from the United States, or any of them.

Before he enter on the Execution of his Office, he shall take the following Oath or Affirmation:—"I do solemnly swear (or affirm) that I will faithfully execute the Office of President of the United States, and will to the best of my Ability, preserve, protect and defend the Constitution of the United States."

SECTION. 2. The President shall be Commander in Chief of the Army and Navy of the United States, and of the Militia of the several States, when called into the actual Service of the United States; he may require the Opinion, in writing, of the principal Officer in each of the executive Departments, upon any Subject relating to the Duties of their respective Offices, and he shall have Power to grant Reprieves and Pardons for Offences against the United States, except in Cases of Impeachment.

He shall have Power, by and with the Advice and Consent of the Senate, to make Treaties, provided two thirds of the Senators present concur; and he shall nominate, and by and with the Advice and Consent of the Senate, shall appoint Ambassadors, other public Ministers and Consuls, Judges of the supreme Court, and all other Officers of the United States, whose Appointments are not

[8] This clause has been superseded by amendment XII.
[9] This clause has been affected by amendment XXV.

herein otherwise provided for, and which shall be established by Law: but the Congress may by Law vest the Appointment of such inferior Officers, as they think proper, in the President alone, in the Courts of Law, or in the Heads of Departments.

The President shall have Power to fill up all Vacancies that may happen during the Recess of the Senate, by granting Commissions which shall expire at the End of their next Session.

SECTION. 3. He shall from time to time give to the Congress Information of the State of the Union, and recommend to their Consideration such Measures as he shall judge necessary and expedient; he may, on extraordinary Occasions, convene both Houses, or either of them, and in Case of Disagreement between them, with Respect to the Time of Adjournment, he may adjourn them to such Time as he shall think proper; he shall receive Ambassadors and other Public Ministers; he shall take Care that the Laws be faithfully executed, and shall Commission all the Officers of the United States.

SECTION. 4. The President, Vice President and all civil Officers of the United States, shall be removed from Office on Impeachment for, and Conviction of, Treason, Bribery, or other high Crimes and Misdemeanors.

ARTICLE. III.

SECTION. 1. The judicial Power of the United States, shall be vested in one supreme Court, and in such inferior Courts as the Congress may from time to time ordain and establish. The Judges, both of the supreme and inferior Courts, shall hold their Offices during good Behaviour, and shall, at stated Times, receive for their Services, a Compensation, which shall not be diminished during their Continuance in Office.

SECTION. 2. The judicial Power shall extend to all Cases, in Law and Equity, arising under this Constitution, the Laws of the United States, and Treaties made, or which shall be made, under their Authority;—to all Cases affecting Ambassadors, other public Ministers and Consuls;—to all Cases of admiralty and maritime Jurisdiction;—to Controversies to which the United States shall be a Party;—to Controversies between two or more States;—between a State and Citizens of another State;[10]—between Citizens of different States;—between Citizens of the same State claiming Lands under Grants of different States, and between a State, or the Citizens thereof, and foreign States, Citizens or Subjects.

In all Cases affecting Ambassadors, other public Ministers and Consuls, and those in which a State shall be Party, the supreme Court shall have original Jurisdiction. In all the other Cases before mentioned, the supreme Court shall have appellate Jurisdiction, both as to Law and Fact, with such Exceptions, and under such Regulations as the Congress shall make.

The Trial of all Crimes, except in Cases of Impeachment, shall be by Jury; and such Trial shall be held in the State where the said Crimes shall have been committed; but when not committed within any State, the Trial shall be at such Place or Places as the Congress may by Law have directed.

[10] This clause has been affected by amendment XI.

SECTION. 3. Treason against the United States, shall consist only in levying War against them, or in adhering to their Enemies, giving them Aid and Comfort. No Person shall be convicted of Treason unless on the Testimony of two Witnesses to the same overt Act, or on Confession in open Court.

The Congress shall have Power to declare the Punishment of Treason, but no Attainder of Treason shall work Corruption of Blood, or Forfeiture except during the Life of the Person attainted.

ARTICLE. IV.

SECTION. 1. Full Faith and Credit shall be given in each State to the public Acts, Records, and judicial Proceedings of every other State. And the Congress may by general Laws prescribe the Manner in which such Acts, Records and Proceedings shall be proved, and the Effect thereof.

SECTION. 2. The Citizens of each State shall be entitled to all Privileges and Immunities of Citizens in the several States.

A Person charged in any State with Treason, Felony, or other Crime, who shall flee from Justice, and be found in another State, shall on Demand of the executive Authority of the State from which he fled, be delivered up, to be removed to the State having Jurisdiction of the Crime.

No Person held to Service or Labour in one State, under the Laws thereof, escaping into another, shall, in Consequence of any Law or Regulation therein, be discharged from such Service or Labour, but shall be delivered up on Claim of the Party to whom such Service or Labour may be due.[11]

SECTION. 3. New States may be admitted by the Congress into this Union; but no new State shall be formed or erected within the Jurisdiction of any other State; nor any State be formed by the Junction of two or more States, or Parts of States, without the Consent of the Legislatures of the States concerned as well as of the Congress.

The Congress shall have Power to dispose of and make all needful Rules and Regulations respecting the Territory or other Property belonging to the United States; and nothing in this Constitution shall be so construed as to Prejudice any Claims of the United States, or of any particular State.

SECTION. 4. The United States shall guarantee to every State in this Union a Republican Form of Government, and shall protect each of them against Invasion; and on Application of the Legislature, or of the Executive (when the Legislature cannot be convened) against domestic Violence.

ARTICLE. V.

The Congress, whenever two thirds of both Houses shall deem it necessary, shall propose Amendments to this Constitution, or, on the Application of the Legislatures of two thirds of the several States, shall call a Convention for proposing Amendments, which, in either Case, shall be valid to all Intents and Purposes, as Part of this Constitution, when ratified by the Legislatures of three

[11] This clause has been affected by amendment XII.

fourths of the several States, or by Conventions in three fourths thereof, as a of Ratification may be proposed by the one or the other Mode Congress; Provided that no Amendment which may be made prior to the Year One thousand eight hundred and eight shall in any Manner affect the first and fourth Clauses in the Ninth Section of the first Article; and that no State, without its Consent, shall be deprived of its equal Suffrage in the Senate.

ARTICLE. VI.

All Debts contracted and Engagements entered into, before the Adoption of this Constitution, shall be as valid against the United States under this Constitution, as under the Confederation.

This Constitution, and the Laws of the United States which shall be made in Pursuance thereof; and all Treaties made, or which shall be made, under the Authority of the United States, shall be the supreme Law of the Land; and the Judges in every State shall be bound thereby, any Thing in the Constitution or Laws of any State to the Contrary notwithstanding.

The Senators and Representatives before mentioned, and the Members of the several State Legislatures, and all executive and judicial Officers, both of the United States and of the several States, shall be bound by Oath or Affirmation, to support this Constitution; but no religious Test shall ever be required as a Qualification to any Office or public Trust under the United States.

ARTICLE. VII.

The Ratification of the Conventions of nine States, shall be sufficient for the Establishment of this Constitution between the States so ratifying the Same.

DONE in Convention by the Unanimous Consent of the States present the Seventeenth Day of September in the Year of our Lord one thousand seven hundred and Eighty seven and of the Independence of the United States of America the Twelfth.

In Witness whereof We have hereunto subscribed our Names,

G[o]. WASHINGTON—PRESID[t].
and deputy from Virginia

[Signed also by the deputies of twelve States.]

New Hampshire

JOHN LANGDON
NICHOLAS GILMAN

Massachusetts

NATHANIEL GORHAM
RUFUS KING

Connecticut

WM SAML JOHNSON
ROGER SHERMAN

New York

ALEXANDER HAMILTON

New Jersey

WIL: LIVINGSTON
DAVID BREARLEY.
WM PATERSON.
JONA: DAYTON

Pennsylvania

B FRANKLIN
THOMAS MIFFLIN
ROBT MORRIS
GEO. CLYMER
THOS FITZSIMONS
JARED INGERSOLL
JAMES WILSON
GOUV MORRIS

Delaware

GEO: READ
GUNNING BEDFORD JUN
JOHN DICKINSON
RICHARD BASSETT
JACO: BROOM

Maryland

JAMES MCHENRY
DAN OF ST THOS JENIFER
DANL CARROLL

Virginia

JOHN BLAIR
JAMES MADISON JR.

North Carolina

WM BLOUNT
RICHD DOBBS SPAIGHT.
HU WILLIAMSON

South Carolina

J. RUTLEDGE
CHARLES COTESWORTH PINCKNEY
CHARLES PINCKNEY
PIERCE BUTLER.

Georgia

WILLIAM FEW
ABR BALDWIN

Attest: WILLIAM JACKSON, *Secretary*

AMENDMENTS TO THE CONSTITUTION OF THE UNITED STATES OF AMERICA, PROPOSED BY CONGRESS, AND RATIFIED BY THE LEGISLATURES OF THE SEVERAL STATES, PURSUANT TO THE FIFTH ARTICLE OF THE ORIGINAL CONSTITUTION [12]

AMENDMENT [I.] [13]

Congress shall make no law respecting an establishment of religion, or prohibiting the free exercise thereof; or abridging the freedom of speech, or of the press; or the right of the people peaceably to assemble, and to petition the Government for a redress of grievances.

AMENDMENT [II.]

A well regulated Militia, being necessary to the security of a free State, the right of the people to keep and bear Arms, shall not be infringed.

AMENDMENT [III.]

No Soldier shall, in time of peace be quartered in any house, without the consent of the Owner, nor in time of war, but in a manner to be prescribed by law.

AMENDMENT [IV.]

The right of the people to be secure in their persons, houses, papers, and effects, against unreasonable searches and seizures, shall not be violated, and no Warrants shall issue, but upon probable cause, supported by Oath or affirmation, and particularly describing the place to be searched, and the persons or things to be seized.

AMENDMENT [V.]

No person shall be held to answer for a capital, or otherwise infamous crime, unless on a presentment or indictment of a Grand Jury, except in cases arising in the land or naval forces, or in the Militia, when in actual service in time of War or public danger; nor

[12] The first ten amendments to the Constitution of the United States (and two others, one of which failed of ratification and the other which later became the 27th amendment) were proposed to the legislatures of the several States by the First Congress on September 25, 1789. The first ten amendments were ratified by the following States, and the notifications of ratification by the Governors thereof were successively communicated by the President to Congress: New Jersey, November 20, 1789; Maryland, December 19, 1789; North Carolina, December 22, 1789; South Carolina, January 19, 1790; New Hampshire, January 25, 1790; Delaware, January 28, 1790; New York, February 24, 1790; Pennsylvania, March 10, 1790; Rhode Island, June 7, 1790; Vermont, November 3, 1791; and Virginia, December 15, 1791.

Ratification was completed December 15, 1791.

The amendments were subsequently ratified by legislatures of Massachusetts, March 2, 1939; Georgia, March 18, 1939; and Connecticut, April 19, 1939.

[13] Only the 13th, 14th, 15th, 16th amendments had numbers assigned to them at the time of ratification.

shall any person be subject for the same offence to be twice put in jeopardy of life or limb; nor shall be compelled in any criminal case to be a witness against himself, nor be deprived of life, liberty, or property, without due process of law; nor shall private property be taken for public use, without just compensation.

AMENDMENT [VI.]

In all criminal prosecutions, the accused shall enjoy the right to a speedy and public trial, by an impartial jury of the State and district wherein the crime shall have been committed, which district shall have been previously ascertained by law, and to be informed of the nature and cause of the accusation; to be confronted with the witnesses against him; to have compulsory process for obtaining witnesses in his favor, and to have the Assistance of Counsel for his defence.

AMENDMENT [VII.]

In Suits at common law, where the value in controversy shall exceed twenty dollars, the right of trial by jury shall be preserved, and no fact tried by jury, shall be otherwise re-examined in any Court of the United States, than according to the rules of the common law.

AMENDMENT [VIII.]

Excessive bail shall not be required, nor excessive fines imposed, nor cruel and unusual punishments inflicted.

AMENDMENT [IX.]

The enumeration in the Constitution, of certain rights, shall not be construed to deny or disparage others retained by the people.

AMENDMENT [X.]

The powers not delegated to the United States by the Constitution, nor prohibited by it to the States, are reserved to the States respectively, or to the people.

AMENDMENT [XI.]

The Judicial power of the United States shall not be construed to extend to any suit in law or equity, commenced or prosecuted against one of the United States of another State, or by Citizens or Subjects of any Foreign State.

PROPOSAL AND RATIFICATION

The eleventh amendment to the Constitution of the United States was proposed to the legislatures of the several States by the Third Congress, on the 4th of March 1794; and was declared in a message from the President to Congress, dated the 8th of January, 1798, to have been ratified by the legislatures of three-fourths of the States. The dates of ratification were: New York, March 27, 1794: Rhode Island, March 31, 1794; Connecticut, May 8, 1794; New Hampshire, June 16, 1794; Massachusetts, June 26, 1794; Vermont, between October 9, 1794 and November 9, 1794; Virginia, November 18, 1794; Georgia, November 29, 1794; Kentucky, December 7, 1794; Maryland, December 26, 1794; Delaware, January 23, 1795; North Carolina, February 7, 1795.

Ratification was completed on February 7, 1795.

The amendment was subsequently ratified by South Carolina on December 4, 1797. New Jersey and Pennsylvania did not take action on the amendment.

AMENDMENT [XII.]

The Electors shall meet in their respective states, and vote by ballot for President and Vice-President, one of whom, at least, shall not be an inhabitant of the same state with themselves; they shall name in their ballots the person voted for as President, and in distinct ballots the person voted for as Vice-President, and they shall make distinct lists of all persons voted for as President, and of all persons voted for as Vice-President, and of the number of votes for each, which lists they shall sign and certify, and transmit sealed to the seat of the government of the United States, directed to the President of the Senate;—The President of the Senate shall, in the presence of the Senate and House of Representatives, open all the certificates and the votes shall then be counted;—The person having the greatest number of votes for President, shall be the President, if such number be a majority of the whole number of Electors appointed; and if no person have such majority, then from the persons having the highest numbers not exceeding three on the list of those voted for as President, the House of Representatives shall choose immediately, by ballot, the President. But in choosing the President, the votes shall be taken by states, the representation from each state having one vote; a quorum for this purpose shall consist of a member or members from two-thirds of the states, and a majority of all the states shall be necessary to a choice. And if the House of Representatives shall not choose a President whenever the right of choice shall devolve upon them, before the fourth day of March next following, then the Vice-President shall act as President, as in the case of the death or other constitutional disability of the President.[14]—The person having the greatest number of votes as Vice-President, shall be the Vice-President, if such number be a majority of the whole number of Electors appointed, and if no person have a majority, then from the two highest numbers on the list, the Senate shall choose the Vice-President; a quorum for the purpose shall consist of two-thirds of the whole number of Senators, and a majority of the whole number shall be necessary to a choice. But no person constitutionally ineligible to the office of President shall be eligible to that of Vice-President of the United States.

PROPOSAL AND RATIFICATION

The twelfth amendment to the Constitution of the United States was proposed to the legislatures of the several States by the Eighth Congress, on the 9th of December, 1803, in lieu of the original third paragraph of the first section of the second article; and was declared in a proclamation of the Secretary of State, dated the 25th of September, 1804, to have been ratified by the legislatures of 13 of the 17 States. The dates of ratification were: North Carolina, December 21, 1803; Maryland, December 24, 1803; Kentucky, December 27, 1803; Ohio, December 30, 1803; Pennsylvania, January 5, 1804; Vermont, January 30, 1804; Virginia, February 3, 1804; New York, February 10, 1804; New Jersey, February 22, 1804; Rhode Island, March 12, 1804; South Carolina, May 15, 1804; Georgia, May 19, 1804; New Hampshire, June 15, 1804.

Ratification was completed on June 15, 1804.

The amendment was subsequently ratified by Tennessee, July 27, 1804.

[14] This sentence has been superseded by section 3 of amendment XX.

The amendment was rejected by Delaware, January 18, 1804; Massachusetts, February 3, 1804; Connecticut, at its session begun May 10, 1804.

AMENDMENT XIII.

SECTION. 1. Neither slavery nor involuntary servitude, except as a punishment for crime whereof the party shall have been duly convicted, shall exist within the United States, or any place subject to their jurisdiction.

SECTION. 2. Congress shall have power to enforce this article by appropriate legislation.

PROPOSAL AND RATIFICATION

The thirteenth amendment to the Constitution of the United States was proposed to the legislatures of the several States by the Thirty-eighth Congress, on the 31st day of January, 1865, and was declared, in a proclamation of the Secretary of State, dated the 18th of December, 1865, to have been ratified by the legislatures of twenty-seven of the thirty-six States. The dates of ratification were: Illinois, February 1, 1865; Rhode Island, February 2, 1865; Michigan, February 2, 1865; Maryland, February 3, 1865; New York, February 3, 1865; Pennsylvania, February 3, 1865; West Virginia, February 3, 1865; Missouri, February 6, 1865; Maine, February 7, 1865; Kansas, February 7, 1865; Massachusetts, February 7, 1865; Virginia, February 9, 1865; Ohio, February 10, 1865; Indiana, February 13, 1865; Nevada, February 16, 1865; Louisiana, February 17, 1865; Minnesota, February 23, 1865; Wisconsin, February 24, 1865; Vermont, March 9, 1865; Tennessee, April 7, 1865; Arkansas, April 14, 1865; Connecticut, May 4, 1865; New Hampshire, July 1, 1865; South Carolina, November 13, 1865; Alabama, December 2, 1865; North Carolina, December 4, 1865; Georgia, December 6, 1865.

Ratification was completed on December 6, 1865.

The amendment was subsequently ratified by Oregon, December 8, 1865; California, December 19, 1865; Florida, December 28, 1865 (Florida again ratified on June 9, 1868, upon its adoption of a new constitution); Iowa, January 15, 1866; New Jersey, January 23, 1866 (after having rejected the amendment on March 16, 1865); Texas, February 18, 1870; Delaware, February 12, 1901 (after having rejected the amendment on February 8, 1865); Kentucky, March 18, 1976 (after having rejected it on February 24, 1865).

The amendment was rejected (and not subsequently ratified) by Mississippi, December 4, 1865.

AMENDMENT XIV.

SECTION. 1. All persons born or naturalized in the United States, and subject to the jurisdiction thereof, are citizens of the United States and of the State wherein they reside. No State shall make or enforce any law which shall abridge the privileges or immunities of citizens of the United States; nor shall any State deprive any person within its jurisdiction the equal protection of the laws.

SECTION. 2. Representatives shall be apportioned among the several States according to their respective numbers, counting the whole number of persons in each State, excluding Indians not taxed. But when the right to vote at any election for the choice of electors for President and Vice President of the United States, Representatives in Congress, the Executive and Judicial officers of a State, or the members of the Legislature thereof, is denied to any of the male inhabitants of such State, being twenty-one years of age,[15] and citizens of the United States, or in any way abridged, except for participation in rebellion, or other crime, the basis of representation therein shall be reduced in the proportion which the

[15] See amendment XIX and section 1 of amendment XXVI.

number of such male citizens shall bear to the whole number of male citizens twenty-one years of age in such State.

SECTION. 3. No person shall be a Senator or Representative in Congress, or elector of President and Vice President, or hold any office, civil or military, under the United States, or under any State, who, having previously taken an oath, as a member of Congress, or as an officer of the United States, or as a member of any State legislature, or as an executive or judicial officer of any State, to support the Constitution of the United States, shall have engaged in insurrection or rebellion against the same, or given aid or comfort to the enemies thereof. But Congress may by a vote of two-thirds of each House, remove such disability.

SECTION. 4. The validity of the public debt of the United States, authorized by law, including debts incurred for payment of pensions and bounties for services in suppressing insurrection or rebellion, shall not be questioned. But neither the United States nor any State shall assume or pay any debt or obligation incurred in aid of insurrection or rebellion against the United States, or any claim for the loss or emancipation of any slave; but all such debts, obligations and claims shall be held illegal and void.

SECTION. 5. The Congress shall have power to enforce, by appropriate legislation, the provisions of this article.

PROPOSAL AND RATIFICATION

The fourteenth amendment to the Constitution of the United States was proposed to the legislatures of the several States by the Thirty-ninth Congress, on the 13th of June, 1866. It was declared, in a certificate of the Secretary of State dated July 28, 1868 to have been ratified by the legislatures of 28 of the 37 States. The dates of ratification were: Connecticut, June 25, 1866; New Hampshire, July 6, 1866; Tennessee, July 19, 1866; New Jersey, September 11, 1866 (subsequently the legislature rescinded its ratification, and on March 24, 1868, readopted its resolution of rescission over the Governor's veto, and on November 12, 1980, expressed support for the amendment); Oregon, September 19, 1866 (and rescinded its ratification on October 15, 1868); Vermont, October 30, 1866; Ohio, January 4, 1867 (and rescinded its ratification on January 15, 1868); New York, January 10, 1867; Kansas, January 11, 1867; Illinois, January 15, 1867; West Virginia, January 16, 1867; Michigan, January 16, 1867; Minnesota, January 16, 1867; Maine, January 19, 1867; Nevada, January 22, 1867; Indiana, January 23, 1867; Missouri, January 25, 1867; Rhode Island, February 7, 1867; Wisconsin, February 7, 1867; Pennsylvania, February 12, 1867; Massachusetts, March 20, 1867; Nebraska, June 15, 1867; Iowa, March 16, 1868; Arkansas, April 6, 1868; Florida, June 9, 1868; North Carolina, July 4, 1868 (after having rejected it on December 14, 1866); Louisiana, July 9, 1868 (after having rejected it on February 6, 1867); South Carolina, July 9, 1868 (after having rejected it on December 20, 1866).

Ratification was completed on July 9, 1868.

The amendment was subsequently ratified by Alabama, July 13, 1868; Georgia, July 21, 1868 (after having rejected it on November 9, 1866); Virginia, October 8, 1869 (after having rejected it on January 9, 1867); Mississippi, January 17, 1870; Texas, February 18, 1870 (after having rejected it on October 27, 1866); Delaware, February 12, 1901 (after having rejected it on February 8, 1867); Maryland, April 4, 1959 (after having rejected it on March 23, 1867); California, May 6, 1959; Kentucky, March 18, 1976 (after having rejected it on January 8, 1867).

AMENDMENT XV.

SECTION. 1. The right of citizens of the United States to vote shall not be denied or abridged by the United States or by any State on account of race, color, or previous condition of servitude.

SECTION. 2. The Congress shall have power to enforce this article by appropriate legislation.

PROPOSAL AND RATIFICATION

The fifteenth amendment to the Constitution of the United States was proposed to the legislatures of the several States by the Fortieth Congress, on the 26th of February 1869, and was declared, in a proclamation of the Secretary of State, dated March 30, 1870, to have been ratified by the legislatures of twenty-nine of the thirty-seven States. The dates of ratification were: Nevada, March 1, 1869; West Virginia, March 3, 1869; Illinois, March 5, 1869; Louisiana, March 5, 1869; North Carolina, March 5, 1869; Michigan, March 8, 1869; Wisconsin, March 9, 1869; Maine, March 11, 1869; Massachusetts, March 12, 1869; Arkansas, March 15, 1869; South Carolina, March 15, 1869; Pennsylvania, March 25, 1869; New York, April 14, 1869 (and the legislature of the same State passed a resolution January 5, 1870, to withdraw its consent to it, which action it rescinded on March 30, 1970); Indiana, May 14, 1869; Connecticut, May 19, 1869; Florida, June 14, 1869; New Hampshire, July 1, 1869; Virginia, October 8, 1869; Vermont, October 20, 1869; Missouri, January 7, 1870; Minnesota, January 13, 1870; Mississippi, January 17, 1870; Rhode Island, January 18, 1870; Kansas, January 19, 1870; Ohio, January 27, 1870 (after having rejected it on April 30, 1869); Georgia, February 2, 1870; Iowa February 3, 1870.

Ratification was completed on February 3, 1870, unless the withdrawal of ratification by New York was effective; in which event ratification was completed on February 17, 1870, when Nebraska ratified.

The amendment was subsequently ratified by Texas, February 18, 1870; New Jersey, February 15, 1871 (after having rejected it on February 7, 1870); Delaware, February 12, 1901 (after having rejected it on March 18, 1869); Oregon, February 24, 1959; California, April 3, 1962 (after having rejected it on January 28, 1870); Kentucky, March 18, 1976 (after having rejected it on March 12, 1869).

The amendment was approved by the Governor of Maryland, May 7, 1973; Maryland having previously rejected it on February 26, 1870.

The amendment was rejected (and not subsequently ratified) by Tennessee, November 16, 1869.

AMENDMENT XVI.

The Congress shall have power to lay and collect taxes on incomes, from whatever source derived, without apportionment among the several States, and without regard to any census or enumeration.

PROPOSAL AND RATIFICATION

The sixteenth amendment to the Constitution of the United States was proposed to the legislatures of the several States by the Sixty-first Congress on the 12th of July, 1909, and was declared, in a proclamation of the Secretary of State, dated the 25th of February, 1913, to have been ratified by 36 of the 48 States. The dates of ratification were: Alabama, August 10, 1909; Kentucky, February 8, 1910; South Carolina, February 19, 1910; Illinois, March 1, 1910; Mississippi, March 7, 1910; Oklahoma, March 10, 1910; Maryland, April 8, 1910; Georgia, August 3, 1910; Texas, August 16, 1910; Ohio, January 19, 1911; Idaho, January 20, 1911; Oregon, January 23, 1911; Washington, January 26, 1911; Montana, January 30, 1911; Indiana, January 30, 1911; California, January 31, 1911; Nevada, January 31, 1911; South Dakota, February 3, 1911; Nebraska, February 9, 1911; North Carolina, February 11, 1911; Colorado, February 15, 1911; North Dakota, February 17, 1911; Kansas, February 18, 1911; Michigan, February 23, 1911; Iowa, February 24, 1911; Missouri, March 16, 1911; Maine, March 31, 1911; Tennessee, April 7, 1911; Arkansas, April 22, 1911 (after having rejected it earlier); Wisconsin, May 26, 1911; New York, July 12, 1911; Arizona, April 6, 1912; Minnesota, June 11, 1912; Louisiana, June 28, 1912; West Virginia, January 31, 1913; New Mexico, February 3, 1913.

Ratification was completed on February 3, 1913.

The amendment as subsequently ratified by Massachusetts, March 4, 1913; New Hampshire, March 7, 1913 (after having rejected it on March 2, 1911).

The amendment was rejected (and not subsequently ratified) by Connecticut, Rhode Island, and Utah.

AMENDMENT [XVII.]

The Senate of the United States shall be composed of two Senators from each State, elected by the people thereof, for six years;

and each Senator shall have one vote. The electors in each State shall have the qualifications requisite for electors of the most numerous branch of the State legislatures.

When vacancies happen in the representation of any State in the Senate, the executive authority of such State shall issue writs of election to fill such vacancies: *Provided,* That the legislature of any State may empower the executive thereof to make temporary appointments until the people fill the vacancies by election as the legislature may direct.

This amendment shall not be so construed as to affect the election or term of any Senator chosen before it becomes valid as part of the Constitution.

PROPOSAL AND RATIFICATION

The seventeenth amendment to the Constitution of the United States was proposed to the legislatures of the several States by the Sixty-second Congress on the 13th of May, 1912, and was declared, in a proclamation of the Secretary of State, dated the 31st of May, 1913, to have been ratified by the legislatures of 36 of the 48 States. The dates of ratification were: Massachusetts, May 22, 1912; Arizona, June 3, 1912; Minnesota, June 10, 1912; New York, January 15, 1913; Kansas, January 17, 1913; Oregon, January 23, 1913; North Carolina, January 25, 1913; California, January 28, 1913; Michigan, January 28, 1913; Iowa, January 30, 1913; Montana, January 30, 1913; Idaho, January 31, 1913; West Virginia, February 4, 1913; Colorado, February 5, 1913; Nevada, February 6, 1913; Texas, February 7, 1913; Washington, February 7, 1913; Wyoming, February 8, 1913; Arkansas, February 11, 1913; Maine, February 11, 1913; Illinois, February 13, 1913; North Dakota, February 14, 1913; Wisconsin, February 18, 1913; Indiana, February 19, 1913; New Hampshire, February 19, 1913; Vermont, February 19, 1913; South Dakota, February 19, 1913; Oklahoma, February 24, 1913; Ohio, February 25, 1913; Missouri, March 7, 1913; New Mexico, March 13, 1913; Nebraska, March 14, 1913; New Jersey, March 17, 1913; Tennessee, April 1, 1913; Pennsylvania, April 2, 1913; Connecticut, April 8, 1913.

Ratification was completed on April 8, 1913.

The amendment was subsequently ratified by Louisiana, June 11, 1914.

The amendment was rejected by Utah (and not subsequently ratified) on February 26, 1913.

AMENDMENT [XVIII.][16]

SECTION. 1. After one year from the ratification of this article the manufacture, sale, or transportation of intoxicating liquors within, the importation thereof into, or the exportation thereof from the United States and all territory subject to the jurisdiction thereof for beverage purposes is hereby prohibited.

SECTION. 2. The Congress, and the several States shall have concurrent power to enforce this article by appropriate legislation.

SECTION. 3. This article shall be inoperative unless it shall have been ratified as an amendment to the Constitution by the legislatures of the several States, as provided in the Constitution, within seven years from the date of the submission hereof to the States by the Congress.

PROPOSAL AND RATIFICATION

The eighteenth amendment to the Constitution of the United States was proposed to the legislatures of the several States by the Sixty-fifth Congress, on the 18th of December, 1917, and was declared, in a proclamation of the Secretary of State, dated the 29th of January, 1919, to have been ratified by the legislatures of 36 of the 48 States. The dates of ratification were: Mississippi, January 8, 1918; Virginia,

[16] Repealed by section 1 of amendment XXI.

January 11, 1918; Kentucky, January 14, 1918; North Dakota, January 25, 1918; South Carolina, January 29, 1918; Maryland, February 13, 1918; Montana, February 19, 1918; Texas, March 4, 1918; Delaware, March 18, 1918; South Dakota, March 20, 1918; Massachusetts, April 2, 1918; Arizona, May 24, 1918; Georgia, June 26, 1918; Louisiana, August 3, 1918; Florida, December 3, 1918; Michigan, January 2, 1919; Ohio, January 7, 1919; Oklahoma, January 7, 1919; Idaho, January 8, 1919; Maine, January 8, 1919; West Virginia, January 9, 1919; California, January 13, 1919; Tennessee, January 13, 1919; Washington, January 13, 1919; Arkansas, January 14, 1919; Kansas, January 14, 1919; Alabama, January 15, 1919; Colorado, January 15, 1919; Iowa, January 15, 1919; New Hampshire, January 15, 1919; Oregon, January 15, 1919; Nebraska, January 16, 1919; North Carolina, January 16, 1919; Utah, January 16, 1919; Missouri, January 16, 1919; Wyoming, January 16, 1919.

Ratification was completed on January 16, 1919. See Dillon v. Gloss, 256 U.S. 368, 376 (1921).

The amendment was subsequently ratified by Minnesota on January 17, 1919; Wisconsin, January 17, 1919; New Mexico, January 20, 1919; Nevada, January 21, 1919; New York, January 29, 1919; Vermont, January 29, 1919; Pennsylvania, February 25, 1919; Connecticut, May 6, 1919; and New Jersey, March 9, 1922.

The amendment was rejected (and not subsequently ratified) by Rhode Island.

AMENDMENT [XIX.]

The right of citizens of the United States to vote shall not be denied or abridged by the United States or by any State on account of sex.

Congress shall have power to enforce this article by appropriate legislation.

PROPOSAL AND RATIFICATION

The nineteenth amendment to the Constitution of the United States was proposed to the legislatures of the several States by the Sixty-sixth Congress, on the 4th of June, 1919, and was declared, in a proclamation of the Secretary of State, dated the 26th of August, 1920, to have been ratified by the legislatures of 36 of the 48 States. The dates of ratification were: Illinois, June 10, 1919 (and that State readopted its resolution of ratification June 17, 1919); Michigan, June 10, 1919; Wisconsin, June 10, 1919; Kansas, June 16, 1919; New York, June 16, 1919; Ohio, June 16, 1919; Pennsylvania, June 24, 1919; Massachusetts, June 25, 1919; Texas, June 28, 1919; Iowa, July 2, 1919; Missouri, July 3, 1919; Arkansas, July 28, 1919; Montana, August 2, 1919; Nebraska, August 2, 1919; Minnesota, September 8, 1919; New Hampshire, September 10, 1919; Utah, October 2, 1919; California, November 1, 1919; Maine, November 5, 1919; North Dakota, December 1, 1919; South Dakota, December 4, 1919; Colorado, December 15, 1919; Kentucky, January 6, 1920; Rhode Island, January 6, 1920; Oregon, January 13, 1920; Indiana, January 16, 1920; Wyoming, January 27, 1920; Nevada, February 7, 1920; New Jersey, February 9, 1920; Idaho, February 11, 1920; Arizona, February 12, 1920; New Mexico, February 21, 1920; Oklahoma, February 28, 1920; West Virginia, March 10, 1920; Washington, March 22, 1920; Tennessee, August 18, 1920.

Ratification was completed on August 18, 1920.

The amendment was subsequently ratified by Connecticut on September 14, 1920 (and that State reaffirmed on September 21, 1920); Vermont, February 8, 1921; Delaware, March 6, 1923 (after having rejected it on June 2, 1920); Maryland, March 29, 1941 (after having rejected it on February 24, 1920, ratification certified on February 25, 1958); Virginia, February 21, 1952 (after having rejected it on February 12, 1920); Alabama, September 8, 1953 (after having rejected it on September 22, 1919); Florida, May 13, 1969; South Carolina, July 1, 1969 (after having rejected it on January 28, 1920, ratification certified on August 22, 1973); Georgia, February 20, 1970 (after having rejected it on July 24, 1919); Louisiana, June 11, 1970 (after having rejected it on July 1, 1920); North Carolina, May 6, 1971; Mississippi, March 22, 1984 (after having rejected it on March 29, 1920).

AMENDMENT [XX.]

SECTION. 1. The terms of the President and Vice President shall end at noon on the 20th day of January, and the terms of Senators and Representatives at noon on the 3d day of January, of the years in which such terms would have ended if this article had not been ratified; and the terms of their successors shall then begin.

SECTION. 2. The Congress shall assemble at least once in every year, and such meeting shall begin at noon on the 3d day of January, unless they shall by law appoint a different day.

SECTION. 3. If, at the time fixed for the beginning of the term of the President, the President elect shall have died, the Vice President elect shall become President. If a President shall not have been chosen before the time fixed for the beginning of his term, or if the President elect shall have failed to qualify, then the Vice President elect shall act as President until a President shall have qualified; and the Congress may by law provide for the case wherein neither a President elect nor a Vice President elect shall have qualified, declaring who shall then act as President, or the manner in which one who is to act shall be selected, and such person shall act accordingly until a President or Vice President shall have qualified.

SECTION. 4. The Congress may by law provide for the case of the death of any of the persons from whom the House of Representatives may choose a President whenever the right of choice shall have devolved upon them, and for the case of the death of any of the persons from whom the Senate may choose a Vice President whenever the right of choice shall have devolved upon them.

SECTION. 5. Sections 1 and 2 shall take effect on the 15th day of October following the ratification of this article.

SECTION. 6. This article shall be inoperative unless it shall have been ratified as an amendment to the Constitution by the legislatures of three-fourths of the several States within seven years from the date of its submission.

PROPOSAL AND RATIFICATION

The twentieth amendment to the Constitution was proposed to the legislatures of the several States by the Seventy-Second Congress, on the 2d day of March, 1932, and was declared, in a proclamation by the Secretary of State, dated on the 6th day of February, 1933, to have been ratified by the legislatures of 36 of the 48 States. The dates of ratification were: Virginia, March 4, 1932; New York, March 11, 1932; Mississippi, March 16, 1932; Arkansas, March 17, 1932; Kentucky, March 17, 1932; New Jersey, March 21, 1932; South Carolina, March 25, 1932; Michigan, March 31, 1932; Maine, April 1, 1932; Rhode Island, April 14, 1932; Illinois, April 21, 1932; Louisiana, June 22, 1932; West Virginia, July 30, 1932; Pennsylvania, August 11, 1932; Indiana, August 15, 1932; Texas, September 7, 1932; Alabama, September 13, 1932; California, January 4, 1933; North Carolina, January 5, 1933; North Dakota, January 9, 1933; Minnesota, January 12, 1933; Arizona, January 13, 1933; Montana, January 13, 1933; Nebraska, January 13, 1933; Oklahoma, January 13, 1933; Kansas, January 16, 1933; Oregon, January 16, 1933; Delaware, January 19, 1933; Washington, January 19, 1933; Wyoming, January 19, 1933; Iowa, January 20, 1933; South Dakota, January 20, 1933; Tennessee, January 20, 1933; Idaho, January 21, 1933; New Mexico, January 21, 1933; Georgia, January 23, 1933; Missouri, January 23, 1933; Ohio, January 23, 1933; Utah, January 23, 1933.

Ratification was completed on January 23, 1933.

The amendment was subsequently ratified by Massachusetts on January 24, 1933; Wisconsin, January 24, 1933; Colorado, January 24, 1933; Nevada, January 26, 1933; Connecticut, January 27, 1933; New Hampshire, January 31, 1933; Vermont, February 2, 1933; Maryland, March 24, 1933; Florida, April 26, 1933.

AMENDMENT [XXI.]

SECTION. 1. The eighteenth article of amendment to the Constitution of the United States is hereby repealed.

SECTION. 2. The transportation or importation into any State, Territory, or possession of the United States for delivery or use therein of intoxicating liquors, in violation of the laws thereof, is hereby prohibited.

SECTION. 3. This article shall be inoperative unless it shall have been ratified as an amendment to the Constitution by conventions in the several States, as provided in the Constitution, within seven years from the date of the submission hereof to the States by the Congress.

PROPOSAL AND RATIFICATION

The twenty-first amendment to the Constitution was proposed to the several States by the Seventy-Second Congress, on the 20th day of February, 1933, and was declared, in a proclamation by the Secretary of State, dated on the 5th day of December, 1933, to have been ratified by 36 of the 48 States. The dates of ratification were: Michigan, April 10, 1933; Wisconsin, April 25, 1933; Rhode Island, May 8, 1933; Wyoming, May 25, 1933; New Jersey, June 1, 1933; Delaware, June 24, 1933; Indiana, June 26, 1933; Massachusetts, June 26, 1933; New York, June 27, 1933; Illinois, July 10, 1933; Iowa, July 10, 1933; Connecticut, July 11, 1933; New Hampshire, July 11, 1933; California, July 24, 1933; West Virginia, July 25, 1933; Arkansas, August 1, 1933; Oregon, August 7, 1933; Alabama, August 8, 1933; Tennessee, August 11, 1933; Missouri, August 29, 1933; Arizona, September 5, 1933; Nevada, September 5, 1933; Vermont, September 23, 1933; Colorado, September 26, 1933; Washington, October 3, 1933; Minnesota, October 10, 1933; Idaho, October 17, 1933; Maryland, October 18, 1933; Virginia, October 25, 1933; New Mexico, November 2, 1933; Florida, November 14, 1933; Texas, November 24, 1933; Kentucky, November 27, 1933; Ohio, December 5, 1933; Pennsylvania, December 5, 1933; Utah, December 5, 1933.

Ratification was completed on December 5, 1933.

The amendment was subsequently ratified by Maine, on December 6, 1933, and by Montana, on August 6, 1934.

The amendment was rejected (and not subsequently ratified) by South Carolina, on December 4, 1933.

AMENDMENT [XXII.]

SECTION. 1. No person shall be elected to the office of the President more than twice, and no person who has held the office of President, or acted as President, for more than two years of a term to which some other person was elected President shall be elected to the office of the President more than once. But this Article shall not apply to any person holding the office of President when this Article was proposed by the Congress, and shall not prevent any person who may be holding the office of President, or acting as President, during the term within which this Article becomes operative from holding the office of President or acting as President during the remainder of such term.

SECTION. 2. This article shall be inoperative unless it shall have been ratified as an amendment to the Constitution by the legislatures of three-fourths of the several States within seven years from the date of its submission to the States by the Congress.

PROPOSAL AND RATIFICATION

This amendment was proposed to the legislatures of the several States by the Eightieth Congress on March 21, 1947 by House Joint Res. No. 27, and was declared by the Administrator of General Services, on March 1, 1951, to have been ratified by the legislatures of 36 of the 48 States. The dates of ratification were: Maine, March 31, 1947; Michigan, March 31, 1947; Iowa, April 1, 1947; Kansas, April 1, 1947; New Hampshire, April 1, 1947; Delaware, April 2, 1947; Illinois, April 3, 1947; Oregon, April 3, 1947; Colorado, April 12, 1947; California, April 15, 1947; New Jersey, April 15, 1947; Vermont, April 15, 1947; Ohio, April 16, 1947; Wisconsin, April 16, 1947; Pennsylvania, April 29, 1947; Connecticut, May 21, 1947; Missouri, May 22, 1947; Nebraska, May 23, 1947; Virginia, January 28, 1948; Mississippi, February 12, 1948; New York, March 9, 1948; South Dakota, January 21, 1949; North Dakota, February 25, 1949; Louisiana, May 17, 1950; Montana, January 25, 1951; Indiana, January 29, 1951; Idaho, January 30, 1951; New Mexico, February 12, 1951; Wyoming, February 12, 1951; Arkansas, February 15, 1951; Georgia, February 17, 1951; Tennessee, February 20, 1951; Texas, February 22, 1951; Nevada, February 26, 1951; Utah, February 26, 1951; Minnesota, February 27, 1951.

Ratification was completed on February 27, 1951.

The amendment was subsequently ratified by North Carolina on February 28, 1951; South Carolina, March 13, 1951; Maryland, March 14, 1951; Florida, April 16, 1951; Alabama, May 4, 1951.

The amendment was rejected (and not subsequently ratified) by Oklahoma in June 1947, and Massachusetts on June 9, 1949.

CERTIFICATION OF VALIDITY

Publication of the certifying statement of the Administrator of General Services that the amendment had become valid was made on March 1, 1951, F.R. Doc. 51–2940, 16 F.R. 2019.

AMENDMENT [XXIII.]

SECTION. 1. The District constituting the seat of Government of the United States shall appoint in such manner as the Congress may direct:

A number of electors of President and Vice President equal to the whole number of Senators and Representatives in Congress to which the District would be entitled if it were a State, but in no event more than the least populous State; they shall be in addition to those appointed by the States, but they shall be considered, for the purposes of the election of President and Vice President, to be electors appointed by a State and they shall meet in the District and perform such duties as provided by the twelfth article of amendment.

SECTION. 2. The Congress shall have power to enforce this article by appropriate legislation.

PROPOSAL AND RATIFICATION

This amendment was proposed by the Eighty-sixth Congress on June 17, 1960 and was declared by the Administrator of General Services on April 3, 1961, to have been ratified by 38 of the 50 States. The dates of ratification were: Hawaii, June 23, 1960 (and that State made a technical correction to its resolution on June 30, 1960); Massachusetts, August 22, 1960; New Jersey, December 19, 1960; New York, January 17, 1961; California, January 19, 1961; Oregon, January 27, 1961; Maryland, January 30, 1961; Idaho, January 31, 1961; Maine, January 31, 1961; Minnesota, January 31, 1961; New Mexico, February 1, 1961; Nevada, February 2, 1961; Montana, February 6, 1961; South Dakota, February 6, 1961; Colorado, February 8, 1961; Washington, February 9, 1961; West Virginia, February 9, 1961; Alaska, February 10, 1961; Wyoming, February 13, 1961; Delaware, February 20, 1961; Utah, February 21, 1961; Wisconsin, February 21, 1961; Pennsylvania, February 28, 1961; Indiana, March 3, 1961; North Dakota, March 3, 1961; Tennessee, March 6, 1961; Michigan, March 8, 1961; Connecticut, March 9, 1961; Arizona, March 10, 1961; Illinois, March 14, 1961; Nebraska, March 15, 1961; Vermont, March 15, 1961; Iowa, March 16, 1961; Missouri, March 20, 1961; Oklahoma, March 21, 1961; Rhode Island, March 22, 1961; Kansas, March 29, 1961; Ohio, March 29, 1961.

Ratification was completed on March 29, 1961.

The amendment was subsequently ratified by New Hampshire on March 30, 1961 (when that State annulled and then repeated its ratification of March 29, 1961).

The amendment was rejected (and not subsequently ratified) by Arkansas on January 24, 1961.

CERTIFICATION OF VALIDITY

Publication of the certifying statement of the Administrator of General Services that the amendment had become valid was made on April 3, 1961, F.R. Doc. 61–3017, 26 F.R. 2808.

AMENDMENT [XXIV.]

SECTION. 1. The right of citizens of the United States to vote in any primary or other election for President or Vice President, for electors for President or Vice President, or for Senator or Representative in Congress, shall not be denied or abridged by the United States or any State by reason of failure to pay any poll tax or other tax.

SECTION. 2. The Congress shall have power to enforce this article by appropriate legislation.

PROPOSAL AND RATIFICATION

This amendment was proposed by the Eighty-seventh Congress by Senate Joint Resolution No. 29, which was approved by the Senate on March 27, 1962, and by the House of Representatives on August 27, 1962. It was declared by the Administrator of General Services on February 4, 1964, to have been ratified by the legislatures of 38 of the 50 States.

This amendment was ratified by the following States:

Illinois, November 14, 1962; New Jersey, December 3, 1962; Oregon, January 25, 1963; Montana, January 28, 1963; West Virginia, February 1, 1963; New York, February 4, 1963; Maryland, February 6, 1963; California, February 7, 1963; Alaska, February 11, 1963; Rhode Island, February 14, 1963; Indiana, February 19, 1963; Utah, February 20, 1963; Michigan, February 20, 1963; Colorado, February 21, 1963; Ohio, February 27, 1963; Minnesota, February 27, 1963; New Mexico, March 5, 1963; Hawaii, March 6, 1963; North Dakota, March 7, 1963; Idaho, March 8, 1963; Washington, March 14, 1963; Vermont, March 15, 1963; Nevada, March 19, 1963; Connecticut, March 20, 1963; Tennessee, March 21, 1963; Pennsylvania, March 25, 1963; Wisconsin, March 26, 1963; Kansas, March 28, 1963; Massachusetts, March 28, 1963; Nebraska, April 4, 1963; Florida, April 18, 1963; Iowa, April 24, 1963; Delaware, May 1, 1963; Missouri, May 13, 1963; New Hampshire, June 12, 1963; Kentucky, June 27, 1963; Maine, January 16, 1964; South Dakota, January 23, 1964; Virginia, February 25, 1977.

Ratification was completed on January 23, 1964.

The amendment was subsequently ratified by North Carolina on May 3, 1989.

The amendment was rejected by Mississippi (and not subsequently ratified) on December 20, 1962.

CERTIFICATION OF VALIDITY

Publication of the certifying statement of the Administrator of General Services that the amendment had become valid was made on February 5, 1964, F.R. Doc. 64–1229, 29 F.R. 1715.

AMENDMENT [XXV.]

SECTION. 1. In case of the removal of the President from office or of his death or resignation, the Vice President shall become President.

SECTION. 2. Whenever there is a vacancy in the office of the Vice President, the President shall nominate a Vice President who shall take office upon confirmation by a majority vote of both Houses of Congress.

SECTION. 3. Whenever the President transmits to the President pro tempore of the Senate and the Speaker of the House of Representatives his written declaration that he is unable to discharge the powers and duties of his office, and until he transmits to them a written declaration to the contrary, such powers and duties shall be discharged by the Vice President as Acting President.

SECTION. 4. Whenever the Vice President and a majority of either the principal officers of the executive departments or of such other body as Congress may by law provide, transmit to the President pro tempore of the Senate and the Speaker of the House of Representatives their written declaration that the President is unable to discharge the powers and duties of his office, the Vice President shall immediately assume the powers and duties of the office as Acting President.

Thereafter, when the President transmits to the President pro tempore of the Senate and the Speaker of the House of Representatives his written declaration that no inability exists, he shall resume the powers and duties of his office unless the Vice President and a majority of either the principal officers of the executive department[17] or of such other body as Congress may by law provide, transmit within four days to the President pro tempore of the Senate and the Speaker of the House of Representatives their written declaration that the President is unable to discharge the powers and duties of his office. Thereupon Congress shall decide the issue, assembling within forty-eight hours for that purpose if not in session. If the Congress, within twenty-one days after receipt of the latter written declaration, or, if Congress is not in session, within twenty-one days after Congress is required to assemble, determines by two-thirds vote of both Houses that the President is unable to discharge the powers and duties of his office, the Vice President shall continue to discharge the same as Acting President; otherwise, the President shall resume the powers and duties of his office.

PROPOSAL AND RATIFICATION

This amendment was proposed by the Eighty-ninth Congress by Senate Joint Resolution No. 1, which was approved by the Senate on February 19, 1965, and by the House of Representatives, in amended form, on April 13, 1965. The House of Representatives agreed to a Conference Report on June 30, 1965, and the Senate agreed to the Conference Report on July 6, 1965. It was declared by the Administrator of General Services, on February 23, 1967, to have been ratified by the legislatures of 39 of the 50 States.

This amendment was ratified by the following States:

Nebraska, July 12, 1965; Wisconsin, July 13, 1965; Oklahoma, July 16, 1965; Massachusetts, August 9, 1965; Pennsylvania, August 18, 1965; Kentucky, September 15, 1965; Arizona, September 22, 1965; Michigan, October 5, 1965; Indiana, October 20, 1965, California; October 21, 1965; Arkansas, November 4, 1965; New Jersey, November 29, 1965; Delaware, December 7, 1965; Utah, January 17, 1966; West Virginia, January 20, 1966; Maine, January 24, 1966; Rhode Island, January 28, 1966; Colorado, February 3, 1966; New Mexico, February 3, 1966; Kansas, February 8, 1966; Vermont, February 10, 1966; Alaska, February 18, 1966; Idaho, March 2, 1966; Hawaii, March 3, 1966; Virginia, March 8, 1966; Mississippi, March 10, 1966; New York, March 14, 1966; Maryland, March 23, 1966; Missouri, March 30, 1966; New Hampshire, June 13, 1966; Louisiana, July 5, 1966; Tennessee, January 12, 1967; Wyoming, January 25, 1967; Washington, January 26, 1967; Iowa; January 26, 1967; Oregon, February 2, 1967; Minnesota, February 10, 1967; Nevada, February 10, 1967.

Ratification was completed on February 10, 1967.

The amendment was subsequently ratified by Connecticut, February 14, 1967; Montana, February 15, 1967; South Dakota, March 6, 1967; Ohio, March 7, 1967; Alabama, March 14, 1967; North Carolina, March 22, 1967; Illinois, March 22, 1967; Texas, April 25, 1967; Florida, May 25, 1967.

---

[17] So in original. Probably be "departments".

CERTIFICATION OF VALIDITY

Publication of the certifying statement of the Administrator of General Services that the amendment had become valid was made on February 25, 1967, F.R. Doc. 67–2208, 32 F.R. 3287.

AMENDMENT [XXVI.]

SECTION. 1. The right of citizens of the United States, who are eighteen years of age or older, to vote shall not be denied or abridged by the United States or by any State on account of age.

SECTION. 2. The Congress shall have power to enforce this article by appropriate legislation.

PROPOSAL AND RATIFICATION

This amendment was proposed by the Ninety-second Congress by Senate Joint Resolution No. 7, which was approved by the Senate on March 10, 1971, and by the House of Representatives on March 23, 1971. It was declared by the Administrator of General Services on July 5, 1971, to have been ratified by the legislatures of 39 of the 50 States.

This amendment was ratified by the following States: Connecticut, March 23, 1971; Delaware, March 23, 1971; Minnesota, March 23, 1971; Tennessee, March 23, 1971; Washington, March 23, 1971; Hawaii, March 24, 1971; Massachusetts, March 24, 1971; Montana, March 29, 1971; Arkansas, March 30, 1971; Idaho, March 30, 1971; Iowa, March 30, 1971; Nebraska, April 2, 1971; New Jersey, April 3, 1971; Kansas, April 7, 1971; Michigan, April 7, 1971; Alaska, April 8, 1971; Maryland, April 8, 1971; Indiana, April 8, 1971, Maine, April 9, 1971; Vermont, April 16, 1971; Louisiana, April 17, 1971; California, April 19, 1971; Colorado, April 27, 1971; Pennsylvania, April 27, 1971; Texas, April 27, 1971; South Carolina, April 28, 1971; West Virginia, April 28, 1971; New Hampshire, May 13, 1971; Arizona, May 14, 1971; Rhode Island, May 27, 1971; New York, June 2, 1971; Oregon, June 4, 1971; Missouri, June 14, 1971; Wisconsin, June 22, 1971; Illinois, June 29, 1971; Alabama, June 30, 1971; Ohio, June 30, 1971; North Carolina, July 1, 1971; Oklahoma, July 1, 1971.

Ratification was completed on July 1, 1971.

The amendment was subsequently ratified by Virginia, July 8, 1971; Wyoming, July 8, 1971; Georgia, October 4, 1971.

CERTIFICATION OF VALIDITY

Publication of the certifying statement of the Administrator of General Services that the amendment had become valid was made on July 7, 1971, F.R. Doc. 71–9691, 36 F.R. 12725.

AMENDMENT [XXVII.]

Article the Second . . . No law, varying the compensation for the services of the Senators and Representatives, shall take effect, until an election of Representatives shall have intervened.

PROPOSAL AND RATIFICATION

This amendment, being the second of twelve articles proposed by the First Congress on September 25, 1789, was declared by the Archivist of the United States on May 18, 1992, to have been ratified by the legislatures of 40 of the 50 States.

This amendment was ratified by the following States: Maryland, December 19, 1789; North Carolina, December 22, 1789; South Carolina, January 19, 1790; Delaware, January 28, 1790; Vermont, November 3, 1791; Virginia, December 15, 1791; Ohio, May 6, 1873; Wyoming, March 6, 1978; Maine, April 27, 1983; Colorado, April 22, 1984; South Dakota, February 21, 1985; New Hampshire, March 7, 1985; Arizona, April 3, 1985; Tennessee, May 23, 1985; Oklahoma, July 10, 1985; New Mexico, February 14, 1986; Indiana, February 24, 1986; Utah, February 25, 1986; Arkansas, March 6, 1987; Montana, March 17, 1987; Connecticut, May 13, 1987; Wisconsin, July 15, 1987; Georgia, February 2, 1988; West Virginia, March 10, 1988; Louisiana, July 7, 1988; Iowa, February 9, 1989; Idaho, March 23, 1989; Nevada, April 26, 1989; Alaska, May 6, 1989; Oregon, May 19, 1989; Minnesota, May 22,

1989; Texas, May 25, 1989; Kansas, April 5, 1990; Florida, May 31, 1990; North Dakota, March 25, 1991; Alabama, May 5, 1992; Missouri, May 5, 1992; Michigan, May 7, 1992; New Jersey, May 7, 1992.

Ratification was completed on May 7, 1992.

The amendment was subsequently ratified by Illinois on May 12, 1992, and by California on June 26, 1992.

CERTIFICATION OF VALIDITY

Publication of the certifying statement of the Archivist of the United States that the amendment had become valid was made on May 18, 1992, F.R. Doc. 92–11951, 57 F.R. 21187.

[EDITORIAL NOTE: There is some conflict as to the exact dates of ratification of the amendments by the several States. In some cases, the resolutions of ratification were signed by the officers of the legislatures on dates subsequent to that on which the second house had acted. In other cases, the Governors of several of the States "approved" the resolutions (on a subsequent date), although action by the Governor is not contemplated by article V, which required ratification by the legislatures (or conventions) only. In a number of cases, the journals of the State legislatures are not available. The dates set out in this document are based upon the best information available.]

PROPOSED AMENDMENTS TO THE CONSTITUTION NOT RATIFIED BY THE STATES

During the course of our history, in addition to the 27 amendments that have been ratified by the required three-fourths of the States, six other amendments have been submitted to the States but have not been ratified by them.

Beginning with the proposed Eighteenth Amendment, Congress has customarily included a provision requiring ratification within seven years from the time of the submission to the States. The Supreme Court in *Coleman v. Miller,* 307 U.S. 433 (1939), declared that the question of the reasonableness of the time within which a sufficient number of States must act is a political question to be determined by the Congress.

In 1789, twelve proposed articles of amendment were submitted to the States. Of these, Articles III-XII were ratified and became the first ten amendments to the Constitution, popularly known as the Bill of Rights. In 1992, proposed Article II was ratified and became the 27th amendment to the Constitution. Proposed Article I which was not ratified is as follows:

"ARTICLE THE FIRST

"After the first enumeration required by the first article of the Constitution, there shall be one Representative for every thirty thousand, until the number shall amount to one hundred, after which the proportion shall be so regulated by Congress, that there shall be not less than one hundred Representatives, nor less than one Representative for every forty thousand persons, until the number of Representatives shall amount to two hundred; after which the proportion shall be so regulated by Congress, that there shall not be less than two hundred Representatives, nor more than one Representative for every fifty thousand persons."

Thereafter, in the 2d session of the Eleventh Congress, the Congress proposed the following article of amendment to the Constitution relating to acceptance by citizens of the United States of titles of nobility from any foreign government.

The proposed amendment, which was not ratified by three-fourths of the States, is as follows:

Resolved by the Senate and House of Representatives of the United States of America in Congress assembled, two thirds of both houses concurring, That the following section be submitted to the legislatures of the several states, which, when ratified by the legislatures of three fourths of the states, shall be valid and binding, as a part of the constitution of the United States.

If any citizen of the United States shall accept, claim, receive or retain any title of nobility or honour, or shall, without the consent of Congress, accept and retain any present, pension, office or emolument of any kind whatever, from any emperor, king, prince or foreign power, such person shall cease to be a citizen of the United States, and shall be incapable of holding any office of trust or profit under them, or either of them.

The following amendment to the Constitution relating to slavery was proposed by the 2d session of the Thirty-sixth Congress on

March 2, 1861, when it passed the Senate, having previously passed the House on February 28, 1861. It is interesting to note in this connection that this is the only proposed (and not ratified) amendment to the Constitution to have been signed by the President. The President's signature is considered unnecessary because of the constitutional provision that on the concurrence of two-thirds of both Houses of Congress the proposal shall be submitted to the States for ratification.

Resolved by the Senate and House of Representatives of the United States of America in Congress assembled, That the following article be proposed to the Legislatures of the several States as an amendment to the Constitution of the United States, which, when ratified by three-fourths of said Legislatures, shall be valid, to all intents and purposes, as part of the said Constitution, viz:

"ARTICLE THIRTEEN

"No amendment shall be made to the Constitution which will authorize or give to Congress the power to abolish or interfere, within any State, with the domestic institutions thereof, including that of persons held to labor or service by the laws of said State."

A child labor amendment was proposed by the 1st session of the Sixty-eighth Congress on June 2, 1926, when it passed the Senate, having previously passed the House on April 26, 1926. The proposed amendment, which has been ratified by 28 States, to date, is as follows:

JOINT RESOLUTION PROPOSING AN AMENDMENT TO THE CONSTITUTION OF THE UNITED STATES

Resolved by the Senate and House of Representatives of the United States of America in Congress assembled (two-thirds of each House concurring therein), That the following article is proposed as an amendment to the Constitution of the United States, which, when ratified by the legislatures of three-fourths of the several States, shall be valid to all intents and purposes as a part of the Constitution:

"ARTICLE—.

"SECTION 1. The Congress shall have power to limit, regulate, and prohibit the labor of persons under eighteen years of age.

"SECTION 2. The power of the several States is unimpaired by this article except that the operation of State laws shall be suspended to the extent necessary to give effect to legislation enacted by the Congress."

An amendment relative to equal rights for men and women was proposed by the 2d session of the Ninety-second Congress on March 22, 1972, when it passed the Senate, having previously passed the House on October 12, 1971. The seven-year deadline for ratification of the proposed amendment was extended to June 30, 1982, by the 2d session of the Ninety-fifth Congress. The proposed amendment, which was not ratified by three-fourths of the States by June 30, 1982, is as follows:

JOINT RESOLUTION PROPOSING AN AMENDMENT TO THE CONSTITUTION OF THE UNITED STATES RELATIVE TO EQUAL RIGHTS FOR MEN AND WOMEN

Resolved by the Senate and House of Representatives of the United States of America in Congress assembled (two-thirds of each House concurring therein), That the following article is proposed as an amendment to the Constitution of the United States, which shall be valid to all intents and purposes as part of the Constitution when ratified by the legislatures of three-fourths of the several States within seven years from the date of its submission by the Congress:

"ARTICLE—

"SECTION 1. Equality of rights under the law shall not be denied or abridged by the United States or by any State on account of sex.

"SECTION 2. The Congress shall have the power to enforce, by appropriate legislation, the provisions of this article.

"SECTION 3. amendment shall take effect two years after the date of ratification."

An amendment relative to voting rights for the District of Columbia was proposed by the 2d session of the Ninety-fifth Congress on August 22, 1978, when it passed the Senate, having previous passed the House on March 2, 1978. The proposed amendment, which was not ratified by three-fourths of the States within the specified seven-year period, is as follows:

JOINT RESOLUTION PROPOSING AN AMENDMENT TO THE CONSTITUTION ON TO PROVIDE FOR REPRESENTATION OF THE DISTRICT OF COLUMBIA IN THE CONGRESS.

Resolved by the Senate and House of Representatives of the United States of America in Congress assembled (two-thirds of each House concurring therein), That the following article is proposed as an amendment to the Constitution of the United States, which shall be valid to all intents and purposes as part of the Constitution when ratified by the legislatures of three-fourths of the several States within seven years from the date of its submission by the Congress:

"ARTICLE—

"SECTION 1. For purposes of representation in the Congress, election of the President and Vice President, and article V of this Constitution, the District constituting the seat of government of the United States shall be treated as though it were a State.

"SECTION 2. The exercise of the rights and powers conferred under this article shall be by the people of the District constituting the seat of government, and as shall be provided by the Congress.

"SECTION 3. The twenty-third article of amendment to the Constitution of the United States is hereby repealed.

"SECTION 4. This article shall be inoperative, unless it shall have been ratified as an amendment to the Constitution by the legislatures of three-fourths of the several States within seven years from the date of its submission."

INDEX

[The terms are cross-referenced to the question numbers in the text. The terms with an asterisk (*) are also included in the Glossary of Legislative Terms in the Appendix.]

○